Lions in the Jungle

Wingate & the Chindits' Contribution to the Burma Victory: February 1943 – August 1944

MARTIN SAMBROOK

First published in 2019 by Chindwin Publishing

Front Cover: General Wingate shortly after his return from Operation Longcloth, 1943, ©Imperial War Museum, IND 2237.

TABLE OF CONTENTS

Preface

Overview of the Burma Theatre

Acknowledgements

Abbreviations

Abbreviations used in References

Chapter One: Introduction and Historiography

Chapter Two: Allies with Divergent Goals

Chapter Three: Operation Longcloth & The Quadrant Conference at Quebec

Chapter Four: Field Marshal Slim and the negative judgement of the Chindits.

Chapter Five: What was the measurable contribution of the Chindits to the Imphal-Kohima battles and Stilwell's advance on Myitkyina?

Chapter Six: Conclusions

Appendices

Bibliography

For the Chindits

Preface

First of all, thank you for reading this book. The fact that you are interested in General Orde Wingate probably suggests at least some knowledge of the history and narrative of Wingate and his officially designated 'Special Force', better known simply as the 'Chindits'. This word is a corruption (unintentionally by Wingate himself) of 'Chinthe', which is a leogryph or lion-like mythical creature, often seen at the entrances of pagodas and temples in Burma and across Southeast Asia. The Chinthe was there to offer symbolic and spiritual protection. It therefore seemed appropriate to use the lion simile in the title of the book.

Whether you have a close family connection to the exploits of the Chindits, or simply an interest in unorthodox aspects of military history, it is certainly a fascinating sub-plot within the story of the Burma theatre of operations; but also, as you will read here in my appreciation, the often neglected aspect of their mission, which had its roots in the fractious Anglo-American negotiations over the global strategy for the defeat of the Axis powers.

My interest in the Chindits has its origins in a chance meeting with two veterans of the Burma campaign, in a Thai restaurant in my home town in Hertfordshire about ten years ago. My first impression before speaking with them was how unusual it was to see two elderly gentlemen, presumably in age somewhere in their mid to late eighties, choosing a spicy curry for lunch. The other unusual aspect to me, was to see an Englishman and an Asian of their generation to be so freely and joyfully revelling in each other's company. They were both attired in their smart blazers with military decorations, and regimental ties. Only later would I learn of the deep friendship and loyalty between British soldiers and the Gurkhas from Nepal, through the many published memoirs of the Chindit campaigns. That friendship and loyalty was clearly evident almost seventy years later.

I initiated a conversation and they proudly recounted an overview of why they were so splendidly turned out; it was for a military reunion. Unfortunately one of their former comrades in arms was too ill to attend so they had come to him, and that was why they were in my home town, enjoying a curry together. Upon asking the inevitable question, 'what did you do in the war?' they proudly replied, 'we were Chindits!'

Regretfully, I had no knowledge of what this meant, and to this day I wish I could revisit this chance encounter knowing what I have learned since. What questions I would've had for them! I did subsequently read about the Chindits in a cursory sense, thinking of them (wrongly) as a guerrilla force and a quite minor part of the overall Burma campaign and war against Japan. Eventually my interest led me to embarking upon a Master's Degree by Research in Military History with the University of Buckingham, under the course leadership of Professor Saul David.

This book is a slightly modified version of my research paper fully titled; *Wingate and the Chindits' Contribution to the Burma Victory: February 1943 – August 1944*. At the outset of my studies I had little idea of just how contentious and bitter this research question was, amongst military veterans and historians alike, both at the time of the Chindits' formation and deployment; but incredibly even through to the present day. The introductory chapter unapologetically goes through an overview of the campaign together with a rather detailed historiography. The way this accepted history of Wingate and the Chindits has developed is critical to understanding both the relevance and importance of their place in the Burma campaign which in this author's view at least, is one that has been deliberately maligned and abused over the last 75 years.

One cannot evaluate Wingate's influence on the Burma

campaign without a detailed look at the actions and attitudes towards both himself and the Chindits, of his superior officer, General Slim, later Field Marshal and Chief of the Imperial General Staff. Slim was rightly beloved and respected by the men of Fourteenth Army, under whom both Wingate and the Chindits served; and together in Burma, they inflicted upon the Imperial Japanese Army its greatest land defeat of the Second World War. My contention here is not to denigrate Slim's achievements but to correct the imbalance of the historic account of the battles of 1944, an account that has been largely attributed to the malicious slights of the *Official History*. My work challenges this account and sees Slim as the main architect and author of what became the *Official History*, largely driven by his own classic account of the campaign, *Defeat into Victory* and subsequent interviews and editorial comment to the researchers and author of the *Official History*.

As for Wingate, my intention is not to excuse his perceived character faults, he was undoubtedly a very difficult man to both please and to manage, whatever your rank. Despite this he did achieve a good deal before being tragically killed early on in his most important contribution to the Burma campaign, in Operation Thursday, in March 1944. I have therefore tried in this book to set aside personal assessments of his character, which are largely incidental to Wingate's ideas and focus on his impact on the enemy, but perhaps even more importantly, his impact on Britain's main ally, the United States, and its executive military leadership, the Joint Chiefs of Staff.

So, what was *Wingate and the Chindits' Contribution to the Burma Victory: February 1943 – August 1944?* You may or may not agree with my conclusions but I do hope that I have at least prompted a fresh evaluation of Wingate and his Chindits, a narrative which seems to be caught in a predictable and somewhat derisory and off-hand assessment by most modern histories of the Burma campaign. The archive materials I have researched have been available for many years but so pervasive is the influence of Slim's account, and that of the *Official History*, that few historians and writers have really looked at the evidence in the spirit of an open and enquiring way. A number of former Chindits and authors have tried to push back, from as far back as the 1950's, and this is covered in some detail in the first chapter; yet the narrative of the *Official History* persists and dominates in most modern accounts.

Regarding the two elderly gentlemen I met some years ago, I would like to think that I do now know what a Chindit was. This book is dedicated to you both, and to General Wingate and all of his fellow Chindits.

Overview of the Burma Theatre

On 15 January 1942, four weeks before the fall of Singapore, the Japanese 15th Army invaded Burma from Siam. The British defence lacked confidence, appropriate resources, suitable tactics and decisive leadership. By 10 May they had been steadily driven back to the Indian border. It was the longest retreat in British military history, and heralded a campaign that lasted more than three and half years before the Japanese forces were themselves pushed back, to the borders of Siam and Malaysia in August 1945.

During the retreat, General Wavell, Commander in Chief India, called for Major Orde Wingate, to see if his skills in unorthodox warfare, developed in Palestine and Ethiopia, could be adopted to useful ends against the Japanese. Wingate was generally unpopular with his officer peers and superiors and this reputation followed him to Burma. He was without doubt a difficult character but Wavell was familiar with his methods in the Middle East and desperate for something to change the unceasing tide of defeat and retreat that dogged the British.

Witnessing the British retreat, Wingate further developed his ideas of Long Range Penetration (LRP), whereby columns of lightly armed infantry would operate deep behind an enemies' front line and attack his Lines of Communication (LoC) which would be poorly defended and vulnerable. In Burma this required British troops to be trained to operate in a jungle environment and abandon the road bound LoC that had made them a poor second best to the Japanese tactics of short hooks though the jungle to the rear of British positions. Almost without fail British defensive lines were abandoned in disarray when a Japanese blocking force appeared out of the jungle astride the British rear position.

Wingate put together and trained a LRP unit, called 77th Indian Infantry Brigade, which consisted of a most ordinary and ageing Liverpool Regiment, the 13th King's, together with Gurkhas, Commandos and Burma Rifles, some 3000 men strong. This brigade became known as the Chindits. The intention was to launch 77th Brigade using LRP tactics deep behind Japanese lines simultaneous with a general advance by the main British forces in Assam. Due to resource constraints, which were a recurring issue in the Burma theatre, all supporting operations were cancelled until only Wingate's force was left. In agreement with Wavell the LRP operation proceeded and operated with modest success blowing railway bridges and railway lines, and killing some Japanese. This was Operation Longcloth, lasting from February – June 1943. A full third of the force was lost to enemy action and many of the remainder too ill to participate further after recuperation in India.

Wingate wrote a report on Longcloth in which he emphasised the positive aspects of the operation whereby ordinary British troops could operate in the jungle successfully against the Japanese. The British military authorities milked the positive propaganda opportunity and Wingate became a popular hero in a theatre that had until now very little to rejoice. His report was sent to Churchill who found Wingate's aggressive qualities a tonic in comparison to the litany of defeats and deferred action. It was also timely as Churchill had to present a proactive military strategy for Burma, under intense pressure from the Americans at the Trident Conference held in Washington in May 1943. The follow-up conference, Quadrant, was due at Quebec in August.

Churchill took the extraordinary step of taking Wingate with him to Quebec to share his tactics and vision of beating the Japanese in Burma. Wingate left the conference with promises of an expanded LRP force, together with an American LRP unit (Merrill's Marauders), and his own dedicated combined air group, which became USAAF 1st Air Commando.

This did nothing to reduce the resistance to Wingate in the Indian Army establishment and he faced an uphill battle with both the British and his own ill-health during the training of this force in readiness for its deployment in March 1944, in Operation Thursday. This was the first Allied mass air assault of the Second World War. Wingate's Special Force, as it was called, was 20,000 men strong and inserted by glider and Dakota landings, 150 miles behind Japanese lines in Burma.

Operation Thursday was launched concurrently with a Japanese invasion into Assam that precluded any supporting British advance. The Japanese invasion was halted at Kohima and Imphal by July 1944 but Wingate's force had taken heavy casualties supporting US General Joe Stilwell's advance on Myitkyina, an important American strategic target to improve the air supply situation to China.

American and British strategies had always differed regarding Burma. For the Americans it was an important base to support Chiang Kai Shek and to keep China in the war, pinning down up to 750,000 Japanese troops. For the British, Burma was simply a difficult and slippery stepping stone, best avoided, if it could be, on the way to regaining the Imperial possessions of Malaysia, Singapore and Hong Kong.

Wingate's operations were lauded in 1944 and he was a national hero. Unfortunately he died in a plane crash two weeks after the launch of Operation Thursday. General Slim, in charge of British Fourteenth Army and Wingate's commanding officer, had a lower public profile and little recognition from Churchill, despite delivering the greatest land defeat on Japanese forces in the Second World War. When Slim's memoirs were published in 1956 and the second and third volumes of the *Official History* in 1958 and 1961, Wingate was castigated as a difficult and unbalanced military leader who squandered men and resources, and made little contribution to the eventual Burma victory.

Former Chindits were incensed and fought for revisions to be made to the *Official History*. Despite some rapprochement in military circles regarding the Chindits, most modern histories of the Burma campaign tend to defer to the Slim and *Official History* narrative regarding Wingate and the Chindit contribution. This study seeks to reappraise the accepted narrative including a critical understanding of the Anglo-American negotiations regarding Burma and the wider strategy for the conduct of the war.

Acknowledgements

I would like to thank Dr Spencer Jones for his advice and guidance in preparation of this study. Thanks also to Professor Mark Stoler, for his perspective of the Anglo-American Alliance, and also Dr Simon Anglim, Wingate expert par excellence. Thanks also to veterans of the Burma campaign who shared their stories with me; Tom Parker, The 1st Cameronians, 90 Column, 111th Brigade, and Richard Day, Royal Welch Fusiliers; the family of the late Mr J.D. Atwell, M.O., 6 Field Ambulance, West Africa Army Medical Corps, 81st West African Division, for access to his private papers, and the members of the Chindit Society who warmly welcomed me to the 75th Anniversary celebrations of Operation Longcloth. A debt of gratitude is also owed to the various archives consulted in researching this book. In particular, I would like to show my appreciation for the wonderful digital archives available in the USA; the FDR Library and the Ike Skelton Combined Arms Research Library, were both of great assistance in assembling relevant and insightful primary source documents. Also, closer to home, the British primary sources available at the National Archives, Kew; the Churchill Archive, Cambridge; and the Imperial War Museum, London.

Last but not least, my thanks to Anita, Joshua and Daniel for patiently listening to my Chindit stories.

Abbreviations

AAF: Army Air Force

ABC1: The secret Washington meetings in 1941 to agree potential Allied strategy in the event of US involvement in WWII, and the accord for a Europe first concept of strategy.

CBI: China-Burma-India

CCS: Combined Chiefs of Staff

CIGS: Chief of the Imperial General Staff

COS: Chiefs of Staff (British)

CSP: Combined Staff Planners

FM: Field Marshal

GHQ (I): General Head Quarters (India)

GOC: General Officer Commanding

HIKOSHIDAN: Japanese Air Division

IJA: Imperial Japanese Army

INC: Indian National Congress

JCS: Joint Chiefs of Staff (American)

JICA: Joint Intelligence Collection Agency

JSM: Joint Staff Mission (Washington)

JSP: Joint Staff Planners

JSSC: Joint Strategic Survey Committee

LoC: Lines of Communication

LRPG: Long Range Penetration Groups

MT: Motor Transport

OPD: Operations Division

S&P: Strategy & Planning Group

SACSEA: Supreme Allied Commander South East Asia Command

SEAC: South East Asia Command

SENTAI: Japanese Air Squadron

Special Force: Wingate's Expanded Force of six LRPG's for

Operation Thursday
USAAF: United States Army Air Force
VLR: Very Long Range (Bomber Force)

Abbreviations used in References

AIR: Air Ministry

CAB: Cabinet Office

CARL: Combined Arms Research Library, Fort Leavenworth

CHAR: Churchill Archives, Cambridge

IWM: Imperial War Museum, London

NARA: National Archives & Records Administration, Washington DC

PREM: Premier

TNA: The National Archives, Kew

USAFHRC: United States Air Force Historical Research Centre

WO: War Office

Chapter One: Introduction and Historiography

The popular image of the Chindits is exemplified by the fictional *Commando Comics'* story of derring-do in the jungle.[1] This appealing narrative sees heroic British soldiers battling Japanese foes in a hostile jungle environment far behind enemy lines. This reflected public assumptions of the superior performance of the Chindits and their eccentric leader, General Orde Charles Wingate, who served as a catalyst to revitalise Fourteenth Army as a whole and transformed the British and Commonwealth soldier in Asia into war winners by 1944-45. This positive image in popular culture was summarised as follows:

The narrative of the Second World War in British comics privileges the role of British and Commonwealth armed forces [...] It focuses on theatres where British and Commonwealth armed forces played a major role – North Africa, Greece, Italy, Normandy, Burma, New Guinea – and on the exploits of famous fighting units such as the Desert Rats and Chindits.[2]

However, a closer reading of the historiography reveals that this compelling and simple story is misleading. The story of Wingate and the Chindits has been filled with controversy from the inception of the force in 1942, its dissolution in 1945 and up to the present day.

The core question of this book hinges on *What was Wingate's & the Chindits' Contribution to the Burma Victory: February 1943 – August 1944*? At the heart of the question is the historical

---

[1] Ashleigh Gibbs, 'Lost Patrol', *Commando,* 4820 (August 1965), 1-63.

[2] James Chapman, *British Comics: A Cultural History* (London: Reaktion Books, 2011), p. 98.

polemic that has developed over the last 70 years that sees Wingate feted as either a 'man of genius and audacity'[3] or demonised as an over - promoted and 'thoroughly nasty bit of work.'[4] The specific dates for this paper's assessment encompass the initial Chindit campaign in February 1943, Operation Longcloth, a standalone raid by 3,000 men organised according to Wingate's developing ideas on Long Range Penetration, and ending with the far more ambitious Operation Thursday, an unprecedented glider borne insertion of 20,000 men up to 150 miles behind Japanese lines in March 1944, wholly maintained by air-supply and close-air support. The remnants of this force were finally withdrawn from Burma in August 1944 and with it the active application of Wingate's ideas of Long Range Penetration came to an end. The surviving Chindit forces that were being refitted and reformed in India were officially disbanded in February 1945.

In order to address the core question it is necessary to look in detail into several important inter-related areas of research that focus on the tangible effects of the Chindits rather than the personality of Wingate and his friction with the British Army establishment. These research questions are:

1. Were the Chindits an expedient but important bargaining chip within the global strategic context of Grand Alliance politics as expressed in the China-Burma-India theatre?

---

[3] The National Archives UK, [Hereafter TNA], PREM 3/143/8, FAR EAST: ANAKIM: Plans for 1944 campaign, July 1943. Winston S. Churchill memo to General Ismay.
[4] *Chief of Staff: The Diaries of Lieutenant-General Sir Henry Pownall,* 2 vols, ed. by Brian Bond (London: Leo Cooper, 1974), II, p. 142.

2. How did the motives of the US and Britain differ and how did Wingate's ideas reconcile these differences?

3. How did Operation Longcloth and its propaganda management shape the expectations of the British and Americans in the lead up to the Quebec agreement on the Burma strategy?

4. In relation to American support of the Chindits, was the direct and contingent contribution of 1st Air Commando significant in attaining air superiority in Burma?

5. What were the conditions and contingencies attached to this American support and why?

6. Was this American support also key to the development of air-land battle tactics, lines of communications and air supply that were so crucial to the eventual Burma victory?

7. Was it as much a personal as a purely military assessment that led to Slim's negative judgement of the Chindits' contribution relative to the resources expended?

8. What was the measurable impact and contribution of the Chindits to the Imphal-Kohima battles and Stillwell's advance on Myitkyina?

A fundamental question to address as a starting point in this book is the divergent understanding and perception of the nature of the second Chindit expedition and the "Special Force" created as a consequence of the agreed objectives of the Quebec Conference in August 1943. The British needed a positive *narrative* to present to the Americans as to British commitment in the China-Burma-India theatre and Wingate opportunistically provided this for Churchill. The Americans needed a tangible military *commitment* from the British to further their interests, specifically in northern Burma, in order to secure a land route to China. Between them, Generals Marshall and Arnold ensured Wingate provided this commitment but not as the British Army in India may have wanted. This difference of intentions may explain the divergent nature of the British and American accounts of Wingate in the secondary literature.

The evolution and development of Wingate and the Chindits is closely bound up in the nature of the Anglo-American Alliance and the deliberations of Grand Strategy across the globe. The many accounts of Wingate that dwell on his perceived deficiencies of character, lack of military capabilities or minimal contribution to the Burma victory tend to overlook the most important consideration in assessing the Chindits; why were they deployed at all in March 1944 and what were they supposed to achieve? They were not deployed at the insistence of Wingate nor were they deployed in direct support of Fourteenth Army. They were deployed at the insistence of President Roosevelt, his Chiefs of Staff; General Marshall and Admiral Leahy and Prime Minister Churchill.[5]

The correspondence between President and Prime Minister in February 1944 was amidst two strategic challenges and choices

---

[5] National Archives and Records Administration USA [hereafter NARA], FDR Library, Map Room Papers, Box 5, FDR to Churchill, February 1944, Personal and Secret from The President for the Former Naval Person No. 479, 23 February 1944; Personal and Secret from The President for the Former Naval Person No. 480, 24 February 1944; Draft notes for The President, Admiral Leahy and General Marshall, 24 February 1944, WHITE 14, 24/2123Z; and The President's approval, BLACK 3 24/ 2322Z, Franklin D. Roosevelt Library and Museum Website; version date 2016. <http://www.fdrlibrary.marist.edu/_resources/images/mr/mr00 30.pdf> [accessed 10 April 2017]

facing the British at this time; firstly the build- up of Japanese forces across the river Chindwin on India's eastern frontier, and secondly Churchill's preference to bypass Burma with Operation Culverin, towards Sumatra and Malaysia. Under the direction of Leahy and Marshall, Roosevelt strongly reminded Churchill that British Imperial interests were of no concern to the United States but the support of General Stilwell in reopening the Burma Road and seizing the airfield of Myitkyina certainly was. Churchill's response was carefully measured, both supportive and contesting American strategy. He wrote:

I can give you the most positive assurances that nothing will be withdrawn or withheld from the operations in North Burma for the sake of Culverin. I have telegraphed Mountbatten emphasising this.

Churchill then continues:

General Wedemeyer, who goes to you tomorrow by Air, will be able to explain this position in detail. He will also unfold the facts about the Ledo Road, which show that it cannot be open for traffic, and then only limited traffic, before 1947.[6]

In the event, Wedemeyer's Axiom Mission to Washington got short shrift, and against the wishes of Churchill, Mountbatten and Fourteenth Army, Wingate's Operation Thursday was launched on the night of 5 March 1944.

The fact that Special Force was deployed at the very moment the Japanese unleashed General Mutaguchi's assaults on Kohima and Imphal was an immense logistical headache for

---

[6] Churchill Archives, Cambridge [Hereafter CHAR], CHAR 20/157/117, Prime Minister's Personal Telegram, Prime Minister to President No. 592; CHAR 20/157/104 Reply to President's No. 479 and 480, 25 February 1944.
<http://www.churchillarchive.com> [accessed 1 February 2016]

both Slim and Mountbatten. The Chindits were totally reliant on air support from very limited resources and were expected to provide little direct contribution to Fourteenth Army, as Special Force was up to 150 miles in advance of the front line. Field Marshal Slim's memoirs are harshly black and white on this issue seeing Special Force as primarily a sideshow, led by a difficult and unpopular showman, compared to the real business of Fourteenth Army in defeating the Japanese.[7] With this account by Slim, the defining narrative on Wingate was set.

A survey of the subsequent historiography will highlight why Slim's interpretation is both personal in dwelling on perceived deficiencies in Wingate's character but more importantly was also a very one- sided interpretation of the military and political situation in the early months of 1944.

A Review of the Secondary Literature

The initial heroic image of the Chindits was created in 1943-44 by British propaganda, which lauded their achievements as a means to offset the perception of the Japanese as jungle fighters *par excellence*.[8] The journalist Charles Rolo's colourful but biased wartime account of Chindit operations, which carried the subtitle *The Incredible Adventure*, accentuated this heroic image of the Chindits which was predominant both during the war and for some time afterwards. The dedication in Rolo's book encapsulates the heroic image very well: 'This book is dedicated to Wingate's Raiders – a band of gallant fighters who

---

[7] Field Marshal Viscount Slim, *Defeat into Victory* (London: Cassell, 1956; repr. 2009).

[8] L. Marsland Gander, 'British Jungle Force Kept Japanese on the Run', *Daily Telegraph*, 21 May 1943.

have shown the Jap that he is no longer master of the jungle.'[9] This view of the Chindits persisted for ten years and included Leonard Mosely's hagiography of Wingate, *Gideon Goes to War*, in 1955.[10] A review of Mosely in *Foreign Affairs* concluded it was more an admiring character study than, 'a serious assessment of the unorthodox methods at which Wingate excelled.'[11]

An unexpected challenge to the popular image of Wingate came in 1956 with the publication of Field Marshal Viscount Slim's memoir, *Defeat into Victory*, and this has been the touchstone of the historical debate to this day.[12] As regards Chindit operations he concluded that, relative to the expenditure of men and material, the balance of rewards and contribution to the final victory were in deficit.[13] Slim's criticism of the Chindits did not go without notice. It drew a response from Christopher Sykes in his detailed biographical study *Orde Wingate*, published in 1959, which attempted to assess his character, motivation and leadership qualities.[14] Sykes drew attention to the odd discontinuity of Slim's views in his memoirs and suggested that Slim was not wholly free of prejudice in his account.[15] Unfortunately, the family of the late

---

[9] Charles J. Rolo, *Wingate's Raiders: an Account of the Incredible Adventure That Raised the Curtain on the Battle for Burma* (London: Viking, 1944).

[10] Leonard Mosely, *Gideon Goes to War* (London: Arthur Barker, 1955).

[11] Henry L. Roberts, 'Gideon Goes to War', Book Reviews, *Foreign Affairs*, 34/4 (1956), 496-504.

[12] Slim, pp. 248-249.

[13] Slim, pp. 625-627.

[14] Christopher H. Sykes, *Orde Wingate* (London: Collins, 1959).

[15] Sykes, p. 17.

Wingate, smarting at Slim's memoir, took offense with Sykes's attempts to assess the psychological profile of Wingate and thereafter refused to cooperate with other researchers and historians by denying access to Wingate's private papers.[16]

Despite Sykes's defence of Wingate, Slim's allegations of the wastefulness of Chindit operations remained the dominant theme of post-war writing and was crystallized in the *Official History* volumes of 1958 and 1961, under the direction of Major Woodburn-Kirby. Volume II of the *Official History* was generally balanced in its criticisms of the first Chindit campaign but also with a hint of the personal slights to follow. Kirby concluded that, 'By far the most valuable lesson learnt was that forces could be maintained in the jungle by air supply, demanded by wireless as and when required.'[17]

Kirby added:

In the circumstances there was a risk that his unorthodox views might be over –exploited in the belief that in his methods, and his alone, the road to victory lay and that, not for the first time, a form of private army would result.[18]

By stark contrast Volume III drove home the negative assessments made by Slim and had the effect of polarising much of the subsequent British secondary literature. Important to note is that the editor of Slim's early memoir drafts was Brigadier Michael Roberts, assistant to Maj. Gen. Woodburn-Kirby, the chief researcher and author of the *Official History* series, especially Volume III, which so markedly and personally

---

[16] Sybil Wingate, 'Orde Wingate and His Critics', *The Spectator*, May 29, 1959, 760-762.

[17] Maj. Gen. S. Woodburn Kirby, *The War Against Japan,* 5 vols (London: HMSO 1958; repr. 2004), II, p. 327.

[18] Kirby, II, p. 327.

attacked Wingate.[19] Kirby enraged many Chindit veterans with the words:

Wingate had many original and sound ideas. He had the fanaticism and drive to persuade others that they should be carried out, but he had neither the knowledge, stability nor balance to make a great commander.[20]

The perspective of Slim and Kirby persists and has become the dominant historic narrative. Writing in 2007 Max Hastings dismissed Wingate's contribution in the War against Japan in just five sentences in a narrative spanning 600 pages. The second of those sentences read, 'At one rash moment, Churchill considered making the messianic, unbalanced Wingate C-in-C of Britain's entire eastern army.'[21]

The verdict of the *Official History* drew criticism from several officers who had participated in Chindit operations. Major-General Derek Tulloch, Wingate's loyal deputy during the war, published a counterblast in 1972 which rebutted Kirby's criticisms point by point.[22] Tulloch accused Kirby of misunderstanding the wider strategic mission of Operation Thursday and deliberately misinterpreting Wingate's official correspondence to bolster his own prejudiced and influential *Official History*. Tulloch countered that:

Wingate emphasised that Long Range Penetration was an offensive weapon, and should be employed "as a vital part of the major plan of conquest". These words are of immense importance; they show-contrary to what has been alleged on all

---

[19] Kirby, III, pp. 217-223.

[20] Kirby, III, p. 222.

[21] Max Hastings, *Nemesis: The Battle for Japan, 1944-45* (London: Harper Press, 2007; repr. 2014) pp. 65-66.

[22] Derek Tulloch, *Wingate in Peace and War* (London: Macdonald, 1972).

sides- that from the start Wingate envisaged LRP as part of the general strategy, *not as an end in itself*.[23]

In support of Tulloch, a new edition of Brigadier Michael Calvert's *Prisoners of Hope* was published in 1971.[24] Calvert was the fighting embodiment of Wingate's ideas and his book detailed the strategic and tactical successes, in his view, of Operation Thursday. In Calvert's words the essence of Special Force was that:

We were a well – balanced fighting force, 20,000 or more men, all potential Jap-killers and no hangers- on, going to the hub of the situation in order that we might cut some of the spokes. Then with pressure on the rim, the whole structure might break down. Thus Special Force in itself was only part of a grander design.[25]

First published in 1952, the book was updated to include Japanese sources which testified to Wingate's impact, which had not been available for his first edition. These same sources had been selectively edited by Kirby in the *Official History* to remove any Japanese praise for Wingate.[26]

With Tulloch's death in 1974, the defence of Wingate was taken up in the pages of *The Journal of Contemporary History*

---

[23] Tulloch, p. 62.

[24] Michael Calvert, *Prisoners of Hope* (London: Cape, 1952; repr. 1971).

[25] Calvert, p. 16.

[26] Combined Arms Research Library, USA [Hereafter CARL], *Japanese Monograph 134*, Burma Operations Record, 15th Army Operations in Imphal Area and Withdrawal to Northern Burma (Tokyo: Headquarters United States Army, Japan Oct 1952; repr. 1957).
<http://cgsc.contentdm.oclc.org/cdm/ref/collection/p4013coll8/id/2605> [accessed 29 March 2016]

with Peter Mead's 'Orde Wingate and the Official Historians'.[27] Mead was highly critical of the *Official History* for its bias and malign influence, which was based on Kirby's personal opinion rather than fact. Mead asserted that the official history had a duty to be impartial because of its status and its influence on future researchers. Unfortunately, Mead's warning on the bias of the *Official History* has often been ignored. For example, Russell Miller's recent biography of Slim accepts Kirby's assessment of Wingate without context or comment.[28] Mead's arguments were developed into a full-length book, *Orde Wingate and the Historians*, released in 1987.[29] Mead also quotes Sir Robert Thompson at length, who had been an RAF ground liaison officer with the Chindits, who unequivocally stated that without the Chindit landings in Operation Thursday, Imphal and Kohima would have been lost. This was repeated in Thompson's subsequent autobiography, *Make for the Hills,* published in 1989.[30] Thomson had also written a foreword in Tulloch's book and worked with Mead in an unsuccessful effort to get the Cabinet Office to correct the *Official History*.

However, Mead was challenged by Brigadier Shelford Bidwell in the pages of *The Journal of Contemporary History*. Bidwell pointed out some of the mistakes that Wingate made in

---

[27] Peter Mead, 'Orde Wingate & the Official Historians', *Journal of Contemporary History*, 14/1 (Jan 1979), 55-82.
[28] Russell Miller, *Uncle Bill: The Authorised Biography of Field Marshal Viscount Slim* (London: Weidenfeld & Nicolson, 2013).
[29] Peter Mead, *Orde Wingate and the Historians* (London: Merlin, 1987).
[30] Sir Robert Thompson, *Make for the Hills* (London: Leo Cooper, 1989), p. 74.

the period leading up to and including Operation Thursday.[31] Bidwell's views, published in 1979, are well - balanced and set in the context of the competing politics and strategies of London, Washington, Delhi and Chungking which resulted in the commitment of Special Force in March 1944 as a practically stand-alone force with none of the supporting British or Chinese forces hitherto promised.[32] Bidwell also assigned motive for Kirby's character assassination of Wingate to a desire for vengeance rather than an impartial assessment of historical facts[33]

It is this global strategic context, as expounded by Bidwell, that many accounts of Wingate and the Chindits fail to appreciate; in particular the wider perspective of his contribution to Allied cooperation in a theatre where there was deep mistrust and misunderstanding between the British and American strategists. Wingate's contribution, whether he was fully cognisant of it or not, in squaring this problem is an area that is little researched or appreciated and will be examined within this assessment.

A review of the post-1980 literature, encompassing the wider military histories of the Burma campaign, shows that authors mostly polarise towards Slim or Wingate in their assessment. This is reflective of the fracture of interpretation created by Slim's memoirs and reinforced by Kirby's *Official History*.

Amongst the general histories of the Burma campaign Louis Allen's *The Longest War* is perhaps the most balanced

---

[31] Shelford Bidwell, 'Wingate and the Official Historians: An Alternative View', *Journal of Contemporary History*, 15/2 (April 1980), 245-256.

[32] Shelford Bidwell, *The Chindit War: Stilwell, Wingate, and the Campaign in Burma: 1944* (New York: MacMillan, 1979).

[33] Bidwell, *The Chindit War*, p. 40.

overview. Allen recognised the harshness of the verdict of Kirby, but was not uncritical of Wingate. He did however, recognise that Wingate was a central and essential part of the story that led to eventual victory.[34] Jon Latimer's history, *Burma, the Forgotten War,* erred towards Slim and Kirby in its assessment of the Chindits.[35]   By stark contrast, Frank McLynn's *The Burma Campaign: Disaster into Triumph 1942-45,* in 2011, is more caustic and scathing about Wingate's character than anything Kirby wrote.[36] Many of the cues in McLynn's attack on Wingate are to be found in both *Defeat into Victory* and the *Official History,* showing the endurance of these historical interpretations.

A typical excerpt of the McLynn Narrative is as follows:

Few public figures have ever been more overtly and blatantly arrogant than Wingate. He assigned himself the status of "great soldier" on the basis of his work in Ethiopia; he habitually used the word "shall" in his orders, implying the command came from a godlike figure; when he could not get from the Indian army 100 per cent of what he had demanded, he wrote back: "Inability is a sign of incapability"[…]Wingate exhibited most of the classic signs of paranoia, from delusions of grandeur to a feeling that there was a general conspiracy to do him down and minimise his talents […] Another classic sign of his religious mania, apart from paranoia, is a relish for violence, in line with the activities of the "smiting" Yahweh of the Old Testament.[37]

Interest in Wingate grew during the 1990s, perhaps as a

---

[34] Louis Allen, *Burma: The Longest War, 1941-45* (London: J. M. Dent, 1984; repr. 1986).

[35] Jon Latimer, *Burma: The Forgotten War* (London: John Murray, 2004).

[36] Frank McLynn, *The Burma Campaign: Disaster into Triumph 1942-45* (London: Random House, 2011).

[37] McLynn, pp. 76-77.

consequence of the approaching fifty-year anniversary of his death. The first new appreciation came from an Indian writer, Colonel Prithvi Nath, with a short book, *Wingate: His Relevance to Contemporary Warfare*.[38] Nath's assessment was that the contribution of the Chindits was significant to the battles of Imphal and Kohima in terms of the enemy resources diverted from the main battle.

David Rooney sought to overturn the influence of Kirby in *Burma Victory: Imphal, Kohima and the Chindit Issue*.[39] This was followed up with a more detailed work, *Wingate and the Chindits: Redressing the Balance*, which detailed the Japanese forces and resources diverted or destroyed by Operation Thursday.[40] A shorter synthesis of his arguments was published in an article for *History Today* in 1994. In this article Rooney points out that no other senior officer, however incompetent in his handling of British or Allied Forces 1942-45, was treated in the same disparaging way as Wingate within the *Official History* series.[41]

In 1995 Trevor Royle published a pro-Wingate biography, *Orde Wingate, Irregular Soldier*, which incorporated much of the post- Kirby debate. Royle acknowledged Wingate's difficult character and unorthodox military methods but concluded that he pioneered the air-land battle tactics so crucial to the Burma victory and had made a more decisive contribution

---

[38] Prithvi Nath, *Wingate: His Relevance to Contemporary Warfare* (New Delhi: Sterling, 1990).

[39] David Rooney, *Burma Victory: Imphal, Kohima and the Chindit Issue, March 1944 to May 1945* (London: Arms & Armour, 1992).

[40] David Rooney, *Wingate and the Chindits: Redressing the Balance* (London: Arms and Armour, 1994).

[41] David Rooney, 'A Grave Injustice: Wingate and the Establishment', *History Today*, March 1994, 11-13.

than that allowed by Slim.[42] John Bierman and Colin Smith's biography of Wingate published after Royle's adds nothing new to the debate other than a rather melodramatic narrative style.[43]

Simon Anglim has built upon the work of the post–Kirby revisionists. He concluded that Wingate was perhaps not as unorthodox as has been assumed by earlier historians and was far more adaptive of existing British Army tactics prevalent in controlling its colonial territories.[44] This was developed into a longer form publication in which Anglim also hints at the potential lessons Wingate's methods hold for counter - insurgency warfare in the twenty first century.[45]

It may also be that the personal animosity between Slim and Wingate was a prime driver of how the British historical narrative has unfolded. Simon Anglim, in personal correspondence, goes so far as to suggest that from his own research of Slim and Wingate's wartime written exchanges, in the Slim Papers held at the Churchill Archive in Cambridge, it is clear that they detested each other.[46] If this is the case it puts a different gloss on Slim's ostensibly balanced and much lauded memoirs and bears further research as to his deeper motive in

---

[42] Trevor Royle, *Orde Wingate: A Man of Genius 1903-1944,* previously published as *Orde Wingate, Irregular Soldier* (London: Weidenfeld & Nicolson, 1995; repr. 2010).

[43] John Bierman & Colin Smith, *Fire in the Night: Wingate of Burma, Ethiopia, and Zion* (London: MacMillan, 1999).

[44] Simon J. Anglim, 'Orde Wingate & the British Army 1922-1944: Military Thought & Practice Compared & Contrasted' (unpublished doctoral thesis, University of Wales, 2007).

[45] Simon J. Anglim, *Orde Wingate: Unconventional Warrior - from the 1920s to the Twenty-First Century* (Barnsley: Pen & Sword, 2014).

[46] Dr. Simon J. Anglim, personal correspondence, 29 April 2016.

his assessment of Wingate in 1956, and alluded to by Sykes in 1958. Brian Bond draws attention to Slim's awareness of his own lack of public appreciation in the years immediately after the war, particularly the sense that his central contribution had been squeezed out by the larger and more appealing characters of Mountbatten and Wingate. With willing collaborators in Roberts and Kirby, who had an agenda of their own, Slim offered his own biased perspective with *Defeat into Victory*.[47]

In summary, it is in the contrasting personalities of Slim and Wingate, and the resulting individual loyalties to them, which has unfortunately obscured and to some degree buried, the real value and contribution of the Chindits to the eventual success of the Burma campaign.

In contrast to the British literature, American authors who have studied the Burma campaign have tended to ground their work in a military perspective and remained aloof from the clash of personalities which has defined the British historiography. The American histories of Wingate and the Chindits, with the exception of Raymond Callahan's, *Burma: 1942-45*, tend to be more measured and generous with little of the Slim or Kirby vitriol that so marks the British accounts.[48] Although Callahan recognized the central importance of Wingate in getting American resources committed to Burma, arguably a key platform for victory, he defaults to the Slim and Kirby assessment of his contribution to that final victory.[49]

---

[47] Brian Bond, 'The Army Level of Command: General Sir William Slim and Fourteenth Army in Burma', in *British and Japanese Military Leadership in the Far Eastern War 1941-4,* ed. by Brian Bond and Kyoichi Tachikawa (Abingdon: Routledge, 2012), pp. 38-52.

[48] Raymond Callahan, *Burma: 1942-45* (Cranbury, NJ: Associated University Presses, 1979), p. 139.

[49] Raymond Callahan, 'The Strange Case of the Prime

The earliest comprehensive account of the China-Burma-India theatre from an American perspective is Charles Romanus and Riley Sunderland's three volume history written under the auspices of the Pentagon to form a United States Army official history.[50] Focusing primarily on General Joseph Stilwell's contribution and impact on events, it covers Wingate in relatively sympathetic terms. The second volume, published in 1956, appeared prior to the works of Slim and Kirby and so misses that perspective. However, that does not explain the plethora of papers and books in the US that focus on the air mission in support of Wingate in northern Burma to assist Stilwell and US strategic interests in China, as officially sanctioned at the Quebec conference in August 1943. This conference led to the creation of USAAF 1st Air Commando, which was to become the transport and close air support artillery of the Chindits. A comprehensive account of the 1st Air Commando and its highly integrated training and operations with the Chindits is found in William T. Y'Blood's, *Air Commando Against Japan: Allied Special Operations in WW2 Burma*.[51]

Minister and the Fighting Prophet', *Finest Hour,* 139 (Summer 2008), 36-39.
<http://www.winstonchurchill.org/publications/finest-hour/finest-hour-139> [accessed on 21 May 2016]

[50] Charles F. Romanus & Riley Sunderland, *Stilwell's Mission to China* (Washington: Department of the Army, 1953); *Stilwell's Command Problems: United States Army in World War II: China-Burma-India Theatre* (Washington: Department of the Army, 1956); *Time Runs Out in CBI* (Washington: Deptartment of the Army, 1959).

[51] William T. Y'Blood, *Air Commando Against Japan: Allied Special Operations in WW2 Burma* (Annapolis, MD: Naval Institute Press, 2008).

The US military colleges have produced numerous research and official histories of both the Chindits and the 1st Air Commando. Any influence of Kirby is difficult to detect and this raises a key question of national differences in the historical perception, appreciation and reality of Wingate and the Chindits' contribution to the Burma victory. A good example of this is found in Major Scott McMichael's *A Historical Perspective on Light Infantry*. [52] This is by no means uncritical but it focuses on questions of military tactics and strategy rather than perceived deficiencies of character. The American literature stresses the innovative nature of the combined air–land Allied force, its lasting legacy and lessons for Special Forces and combined operations, its relevance to the challenges of modern warfare, and the tangible results in destroying Japanese forces. Without Wingate's Chindits there would have been no 1st Air Commando, which itself played a major role in crippling Japanese air forces during the lead up to and consolidation of Operation Thursday.

The contribution of the Air Commando to Operation Thursday are also detailed in some of the British histories that focus primarily on the air war such as Christopher Shores' *Bloody Shambles* trilogy, which in its third volume covers the period of the Chindits and the eventual victory of Fourteenth Army.[53] Michael Pearson provides a diary driven account of the air campaign with similar conclusions as to the vital contribution of air power to not just Chindit operations but to

---

[52] CARL, Major Scott Ray McMichael, *A Historical Perspective on Light Infantry* (Fort Leavenworth, KS: US Army Command & General Staff College, 1987). <http://cgsc.contentdm.oclc.org/cdm/singleitem/collection/p16 040coll3/id/10/rec/30> [accessed 8 March 2015]

[53] Christopher F. Shores, *Air War for Burma*, 3 vols (London: Grub Street, 2005).

Slim's whole strategic plan, as it developed from the defence of the Administrative Box in the Arakan in February 1944, through to the final assault on Rangoon in May 1945.[54]

In conclusion, there appears to be a gap in the current literature that properly balances the British and American perspectives on Wingate and the Chindits. This may be a consequence of different strategic interests and perhaps Wingate's main failing in British eyes, is that he served the agenda agreed in Quebec, which furthered American interests better than those of the British. Special Force was not a wholly British endeavour with British goals in mind but an Allied one whose objectives were often in conflict. These conflicts are well documented by Christopher Thorne, especially the divergent views on the Burma strategy as it related to China.[55] A reassessment of Wingate requires acknowledgement of the global and local strategies of the main Allies.

Without exception, all histories of the Burma campaign underline the vital importance of air superiority, air transport, air supply and close air support to forces on the ground. As Slim himself recognised in *Defeat into Victory,* 'Ours was a joint land and air war; its result, as much a victory for the air forces as for the army'.[56] Foremost in this resource build up were the USAAF resources which may not have been available without a belief that the British would fight in Burma, and specifically northern Burma to further US strategic interests rather than British Imperial ones. Wingate stiffened that belief. As Tulloch points out, it was the reputation of Wingate's word in

---

[54] Michael Pearson, *The Burma Air Campaign 1941-1945* (Barnsley: Pen & Sword, 2006).
[55] Christopher Thorne, *Allies of a Kind* (London: Hamish Hamilton, 1978), pp. 305-327.
[56] Slim, p. 624.

Washington that secured vital additional air transport in April 1944.[57] This paper will further assess Wingate's contribution to the Allied cooperation that led to the eventual Burma victory and is overlooked by so many of the British accounts.

The available literature, particularly on the British side, is heavy on personality and prejudice. There is an opportunity to reach beyond the 70-year-old war of words around the two enormously strong personalities of Slim and Wingate to assess the real political and strategic contribution Special Force made, not just the immediate military significance or perceived deficiencies of personal character.

---

[57] Tulloch, p. 225.

Chapter Two: Allies with Divergent Goals

'Running a war seems to consist in making plans and ensuring that all those destined to carry it out don't quarrel with each other instead of the enemy.'[58]

With this overview of the various themes in the historiography we can see that the conventional interpretation of the Chindits as a mere sideshow is a contestable one and ignores the enormous differences in not just the military goals, but foremost, the differences in the political and strategic objectives between the Allies. In order to understand the rationale of these objectives it is necessary to examine the decisions made by the US Joint Chiefs of Staff in Washington, their opposite numbers on the British Chiefs of Staff, and the compromises made amongst them as the Anglo- American Combined Chiefs of Staff, not forgetting their own political leaders personal prejudices and preferences in Roosevelt and Churchill. This section will explore two main themes:

1. Were the Chindits an expedient but important bargaining chip within the global strategic context of Grand Alliance politics as expressed in the China-Burma-India theatre?

2. How did the motives of the US and Britain differ and how did Wingate's ideas reconcile these differences?

Although the allocation of the Special Force mission was well documented and understood from the Quadrant conference in Quebec in August 1943, the knotty problem of Allied policy

---

[58] Field Marshal Lord Alanbrooke, *War Diaries 1939-45*, ed. by Alex Danchev & Daniel Todman (London: Weidenfeld & Nicolson, 2001), p. 400.

differences in Burma traces back to the Casablanca conference in January 1943 and before this to the difficult discussions between the Combined Chiefs of Staff through the summer and autumn of 1942 regarding the sacrosanctity of the 'Germany first' strategy (rather than Japan and the Pacific) and the American-Soviet push for an early cross- Channel assault in 1942-43 ('Bolero', 'Sledgehammer' and 'Roundup') in the lead up to the Torch landings ('Gymnast') in North Africa on 8 November 1942.

Reflecting on the acrimonious Allied discussions of 1942 in the run up to Torch in November, Lord Ismay, Churchill's Chief of Staff wrote:

Everyone agreed that the death- blow to Germany must be delivered across the Channel. In fact everyone seemed to agree with the American proposals in their entirety. No doubts were expressed; no discordant note struck. It is easy to be wise after the event, but perhaps it would have obviated future misunderstandings if the British had expressed their views more frankly [...] But nothing of the kind was said, and the upshot of the meeting was that the Defence Committee accepted the proposals in principle, with the single, and not very relevant, reservation that sufficient strength must be maintained in the East to prevent a junction between the Japanese and the Germans.[59]

British commitment to this cross - Channel strategy at the earliest opportunity was the lens for viewing most if not all subsequent global strategic decisions and operations to a greater or lesser extent, especially Burma. Here it was that the promises of amphibious resources for elaborate combined operations never materialised, with shipping and landing craft always

---

[59] Lord Ismay, *The Memoirs of Lord Ismay* (London: Heinemann, 1960), pp. 249-250.

prioritised and diverted for Africa, Sicily, Italy and France, or kept for the main Pacific thrusts by Nimitz and MacArthur.

The converging currents of Allied opinion and debate on desired strategy in CBI were always complex and hardly clearer with the appointment of Mountbatten as Supreme Allied Commander South East Asia. To make sense of both the Longcloth and Thursday missions in 1943 and 1944 it is necessary to look at these different currents and the impact they had on shaping events in Burma. At the highest levels of strategy making, in the continual deliberations of the CCS, the US JCS and directly between Roosevelt and Churchill, numerous decisions both directly and indirectly affected Burma due to:

1. American mistrust of British political and Imperial ambitions generally and specifically in regards to Burma and South East Asia. This issue even manifested itself in the making of wartime propaganda movies. A joint movie on the Burma campaign in 1945 became two separate movies; David MacDonald & Roy Boulting, *Burma Victory* (1945) and Frank Capra, *The Stilwell Road* (1945), since the Americans did not want to be seen supporting Imperial British objectives.[60]

2. American focus on China as a key strategic component in initially holding Japan defensively and subsequently building up resources and taking the war to Japan offensively.

3. Roosevelt's commitment to building up China and Generalissimo Chiang Kai Shek as a foremost member of the post - war new world order.

---

[60] James Chapman, *The British at War: Cinema, State and Propaganda, 1939-45* (London: Tauris, 1998), pp. 153-154.

4. Antipathy and suspicion between the British and Chinese authorities over each other's spheres of political and military interest.

5. Resource constraints on munitions and shipping, in particular landing craft, committed to other theatres by the 'Germany first' strategy agreed at the Arcadia Conference in 1941 and adhered to for the war's duration, despite threats to shift to a Pacific first emphasis by the JCS.

6. American impatience with a perceived British reluctance to fully engage the enemy either in France or Burma in 1943 and the overall mistrust of intentions from the strategic disputes in 1942.

7. The corrosive influence of General Joseph Stilwell on relations with both the British and Chinese. "Vinegar Joe" was a trusted protégé and personal friend of General George C. Marshall, the Head of the JCS. Stilwell it might be added also disagreed with the US policy, or more specifically, Roosevelt's and the Generalissimo's, of backing General Clare Chennault's Air Volunteer Group as the best bet to achieve its objectives in China.

8. Stalin's call for a 'Second Front' and American concerns for protecting Russia's flank in Asia from a Japanese attack in lieu of this much delayed 'Second Front'.

9. American focus on the logistics and timing of operations across the two main theatres of Europe and the Pacific together with the domestic political pressures of a speedy conclusion and victory in both.

10. American strategy that saw the wars against Germany and Japan as primarily parallel campaigns versus a British one of seeing the theatres as sequential events

which focused the allied differences around timing, commitment and offensive action.

It is the confluence of these pressures at different times and in varying weight that committed the Chindits to battle in both 1943 and 1944 but especially the latter Operation Thursday in March 1944. This operation was primarily to support US interests in northern Burma and China, such that overall control of Special Force was handed over to Stilwell after Wingate's death just two weeks into the operation. It is no coincidence that the Chindits were primarily equipped by the US, true enough of many British forces, but Wingate was given practically carte blanche on equipment by the Americans in the wake of the Quadrant agreement, in a theatre so obviously starved of resources. In addition to this Arnold and Marshall provided a dedicated air resource with the specially created 1st Air Commando jointly led by two outstanding and highly decorated USAAF officers, Colonel Philip Cochran and Colonel John Alison.

Mountbatten's official post war Report on SEAC operations to the CCS recounts a typically vain and self -important estimation of his own role in the securing a commitment from General Arnold the resources of 1st Air Commando. This is a denial of the true nature of what the British had actually agreed to undertake in northern Burma. [61] Rather, it is argued here that the Americans had placed a heavy insurance bet on making sure the British delivered in northern Burma and that explains the largesse in the provision of 1st Air Commando from General Arnold and General Marshall. It was not a gift, it was to put the

---

[61] Vice Admiral the Earl Mountbatten of Burma, *Report to the Combined Chiefs of Staff by the Supreme Allied Commander South East Asia, 1943-1945* (London: HMSO, 1951), p. 4.

British where the JCS wanted them to assist Stilwell and deliver American strategic goals in China. In a post-war interview with his official biographer, Marshall was to recount his determination not to see the resources of 1st Air Commando shared amongst the British forces but to be dedicated to Wingate's mission. This reference by Marshall reveals his palpable irritation with what he and many in the US forces saw as British lassitude in prosecuting an aggressive posture in the CBI theatre. He wanted the resources so generously given actually used in the Allied cause as shaped through the prism of American objectives and priorities:

I […] warned everybody that if they took anything from the operations (Stilwell, the British, and the Chinese all wanted some of the stuff I had allotted for Wingate), I would take it back.[62]

Wingate clearly made a significant impression on General Marshall. From his personal interviews with Marshall, his biographer Pogue, calls out just two names to highlight Marshall's admiration of fighting soldiers who go beyond the normal and push the extremities of endurance and effort to get the job done. Two officers from the same theatre, Stilwell and Wingate.[63]

Charles Brower's *Defeating Japan: The Joint Chiefs of Staff and Strategy in the Pacific War,* assesses the dual importance of both political and military considerations in evolution of the JCS strategy from a US perspective at the Casablanca, Trident,

---

[62] Forrest C. Pogue, *George C. Marshall*, 4 vols (New York: Viking Press, 1973), III, p. 257.

[63] Pogue, II, p. 406.

Quadrant and Sextant conferences in 1943.[64] Brower suggests that the JCS were deliberately manoeuvring the British to action in support of US military and political objectives in China and Burma that were contrary to British desired military and political policy. In Brower's view the price to the British of a Mediterranean first strategy in 1943 and delays for Bolero and Roundup   (the cross channel assault), until 1944, was to support the US strategy for the defeat of Japan primarily via the maintenance of China (or more specifically Chiang Kai Shek), securing northern Burma to reopen the Burma Road and securing the air supply route from Assam to Chungking from Japanese air attack. Brower asserts that:

The special American relationship with China guaranteed a dominant American voice in settling matters with Britain in Far Eastern matters. Despite nominal British jurisdiction over the area west of Singapore, American assertiveness in strategic matters extended in practice even to Burma, a country whose re-conquest was requisite to ending the blockade of China [...] British actions required the approval of the Combined Chiefs of Staff. Since the combined chiefs acted only on the basis of unanimity, the effect was to increase American strategic leverage in that "British" theatre [...] as the war continued its incessant demands on British resources, the JCS came to dominate in all matters in the war against Japan that they deemed important.[65]

It is in this context of the needs of global strategy and compromise between the Allies that the commitment of Special Force and the inherent limitations and contradictions of that

---

[64] Charles F Brower, *Defeating Japan: The Joint Chiefs of Staff and Strategy in the Pacific War, 1943-1945* (New York: Palgrave Macmillan, 2012; repr. as an e-book).
[65] Brower, p. 5.

strategy and its military results, as officially deployed in Burma, that the Chindit campaign must be understood.

The British were very much on the hook approaching Quadrant in August 1944 for a coherent plan to present to the Americans on how the British would further the policy objectives of Roosevelt in China and the JCS interpretation of the strategy required to deliver the President's policy. Against a backdrop of utter defeat of British arms in South East Asia in 1942, the debacle of the Arakan offensive in Burma in February 1943, combined with the general recalcitrant attitude of the British forces in India to engage the Japanese, the modest exploits of Wingate's Longcloth raid in February – May 1943 was embraced by Churchill. Here was a narrative for positive action and commitment by the British to further American strategy, much against the wishes of the Indian Army establishment.

The Symbol Conference at Casablanca

In January 1943, in the approach to the Casablanca conference, the Americans were clear that they needed both an American united front and agenda to force the British into action in the CBI theatre and this is clear from the minutes of both the Conference and the pre –meeting minutes of the JCS.[66] The attitudes of the JCS displayed in these minutes were to constantly resurface throughout Allied conferences of 1943-44 as the Americans sought to commit the British to substantive action in support of China which was contrary to the preferred

---

[66] CARL, *Casablanca Conference, January 1943, Papers & Minutes of Meetings 1943* (Washington, DC: Office of the Combined Chiefs of Staff, 1943).
<http://cgsc.contentdm.oclc.org/cdm/ref/collection/p4013coll8/id/3688> [accessed 29 March 2016]

British pursuit of strategies of self – interest in India and in its former Imperial possessions of Malaysia, Singapore and Hong Kong, now held by the Japanese.

The following quotes from the minutes of the JCS are instructive as to American views of the British position going into the Casablanca talks in January 1943:

ADMIRAL KING stated that he believed we should discuss world-wide strategy first before getting to specific operations and that we should resist any effort on the part of the British to deviate from this.

GENERAL MARSHALL repeated that he believed that even in the case of world-wide strategy, the British thought would be at all times directed towards Operation BRIMSTONE while he, personally, could not help but have the question of tonnage uppermost in his mind.

GENERAL ARNOLD said that the British were not thinking world strategy but only of the next operation.[67]

Brimstone was Churchill's favoured route into Italy, via Sardinia and Corsica, and these comments neatly illustrate the differences that the US JCS perceived between the Allied strategies during the course of the war. Churchill and his COS were seen as frittering away resources on peripheral and sequential operations, from Norway to the Balkans, the Mediterranean and beyond. To the British, mindful of scarce resources of both manpower and materiel and recent defeats in France and the western deserts, the indirect approach made

---

[67] CARL, Joint Chiefs of Staff Minutes of Meeting Held on Wednesday, January 13, 1943, at 1500hrs, *Casablanca Conference, January 1943, Papers & Minutes of Meetings 1943*, p. 3.
<http://cgsc.contentdm.oclc.org/cdm/ref/collection/p4013coll8/id/3688> [accessed 29 March 2016]

sense. One should of course acknowledge that Brooke as CIGS and the other members of the COS had to severely temper some of Churchill's more fanciful ideas of the indirect approach. To the American military leadership, victory was obtainable only via a head on assault against Nazi Germany at the shortest point of entry, North -West France. Marshall and the JCS were seeking a Clausewitzian decisive defeat in the field of the enemy arms. The British appeared to be avoiding such a confrontation via a series of indirect approaches that would allow for an incremental or emergent strategy to reveal itself. The two approaches are apparent in the minutes of the first two days of the Casablanca conference, as General Alan Brooke and General Marshall verbally sparred and irritated each other. Brooke's diary entries for the Casablanca conference firmly, and unfairly, dismissed Marshall's strategic capabilities.[68]

Having made the defeat of Germany the priority commitment officially as far back as the ABC1 discussions in August 1941, the key difference between the Allied positions was that the British were perceived as looking at the defeat of Germany and Japan as primarily sequential events whereas the Americans saw them as parallel efforts on a 70 / 30 resource commitment and this they believed was the quickest route to final surrender of both belligerents. At the end of 1942 the Americans had a two pronged strategy for the defeat of Japan with pressure to be ceaselessly applied from the Pacific theatre via the forces of Nimitz and MacArthur and from China as the platform for a strategic bombing of Japanese lines of Communication and tying down of up to half a million Japanese troops. The American strategy emerging at Casablanca was one of confidence and that they were the senior partner in the Anglo-American alliance. They had felt out-manoeuvred and out-

---

[68] Alanbrooke, *War Diaries*, pp. 360-361.

negotiated by the British in previous meetings but at Casablanca they were determined to be more prepared with their strategic view and negotiation red lines. For the war against Japan this meant a free hand in the Pacific with minimal or no scrutiny, least of all a veto on the JCS strategy and a bending of British will and resources to apply pressure in Burma in support of the China strategy. In the event, the American service chiefs felt out-manoeuvred yet again by the wily British negotiators at Casablanca, and that Roosevelt had again fallen for the personal approach of Churchill, by-passing the views of the JCS, and committing to Husky, the invasion of Sicily. As Wedemeyer reflected in his memoirs in the aftermath of Casablanca, 'we came, we listened, and we were conquered.'[69]

Brower constantly refers to the time factor as a key constraint on Marshall and the JCS in developing and managing the strategy for the defeat of Japan. Uppermost in their minds was the danger of losing popular support for the full prosecution of the war should the prospect of final victory be forecast to be several years beyond the defeat of Germany, as it was under a number of planning scenarios. To many American planners, including the JCS, the Mediterranean first strategy of Churchill and Brooke was a major drag on the time factor they felt that they were severely constrained by.

Added to this though, was a deeply held conviction in the US military throughout the war, that Britain and the US were not necessarily allies in everything and that their natural reservations about British intentions as an Imperial power were valid questions at all times. Mark Stoler, in *Allies and Adversaries,* exposes the seething discontent within sections of the American armed services at the evolution of Allied strategy

---

[69] Albert C. Wedemeyer, *Wedemeyer Reports!* (New York: Holt, 1958), p. 192.

through 1942-43 which were perceived to be contrary to American military and political interests.[70] It was the direct relationship between Churchill and Roosevelt in this period that imposed a compromise that was grudgingly accepted by the JCS and its wider inter-services strategy and planning organisation. This did not mean they were in agreement with the Mediterranean strategy, they were simply obeying their President's wishes, with deep reservations. This was the prevailing US mood post-Casablanca.

Any doubt about the predisposition of the JCS and its supporting staff planners is laid bare in Stoler's work. Admiral King, the US Chief of Naval Operations was perhaps the best known antagonist of the British on the JCS and the arch proponent of the 'Pacific first' strategy that required firm British commitment in Burma to support American objectives. King had argued in his War College thesis in 1932 that the British 'must be considered a potential enemy and a powerful one, not so much as to questions of security but certainly as to matters involving the growth of our foreign trade, financial supremacy and our dominant position in world affairs.' This was not an isolated point of view amongst the attendees of both American war colleges in the inter war years, with some seeing the United States and Britain as deadly rivals that might go to war themselves.[71]

Prior to Pearl Harbour this sense of Anglophobia and isolationist tendencies was present at the highest levels and permeated the services too at all levels and even the general population reflected this sense of mistrust and dislike of British

---

[70] Mark A. Stoler, *Allies and Adversaries: The Joint Chiefs of Staff, The Grand Alliance, and U.S. Strategy in World War II* (Chapel Hill: University of North Carolina Press, 2000).
[71] Stoler, p. 8.

Imperialism, as opinion polls showed, even after Pearl Harbour.[72] General Marshall himself was not unaffected by this culture of mistrust or wariness of British designs. Marshall was a protégé of General Stanley Dunbar Embick, who was deputy chief of staff and army commander 1936-9. Embick was a leading proponent for isolationism and appeasement with Germany and saw any involvement with Britain in either Europe or the Pacific as contrary to US interests.

Within the military establishment there was a full spectrum of opinion from Anglophiles to Anglophobes and all shades in between. In this former group within the Joint Army-Navy planning staff was an element that warned, 'we cannot afford, nor do we need, to entrust our national future to British direction', as with the British negotiators, who saw post war interests, commercial and military, never absent from mind, 'we would like to safeguard our own eventual interests'. With reservations, this was the group with which Marshall himself most identified.[73]

DC Watt noted of this period that:

In Washington war was being waged with five enemies in descending order of priority: with the army or navy, with the Republican Party, with the British, and thereafter with the Germans and the Japanese. For many in the armed forces [...] it was the third of these which occupied most of their time and thoughts.[74]

In the reorganisation of the JCS machinery at the end of 1942

---

[72] Steve Weiss, *Allies in Conflict: Anglo-American Strategic Negotiations, 1938-44: Studies in Military and Strategic History* (London: Palgrave Macmillan, 1996), p. 8.
[73] Pogue, II, p. 121.
[74] D.C. Watt, 'US Globalism: The End of the Concert of Europe,' in Kimball, *America Unbound,* quoted in Stoler, p. 118.

and early 1943 Embick became the senior army representative of the newly formed Joint Strategic Survey Committee (JSSC), advising on both military and political issues and interests of the US as a coalition partner. In this position his opinions still clearly had the ear and respect of Marshall. As Stoler points out, the appointment of Embick to this senior advisory group of the JCS revealed that the anti-British sentiments within the army had been strengthened by the strategic disputes of 1942.[75] The navy representative on the JSSC was Vice Admiral Russell Wilson, who amongst various other duties had been Chief of Staff to Admiral King. Of all the JCS members, King was the bête noir of the British in the CCS deliberations throughout the war.

Within the Operations Division (OPD) of the US Army General Staff, the recently created Strategy and Planning Group (S&P) was under General Albert C. Wedemeyer, son -in -law to Embick. From 1936-1938 Wedemeyer had attended the German War College as an exchange student and favoured appeasement and US avoidance of a European war. That Wedemeyer shared many of his father –in- law's views is evident in the S&P submissions to the JCS that supported those from the JSSC.[76] It is notable that one of the outcomes of the Quadrant meetings in August – September 1943 was the appointment of Wedemeyer as Chief of Staff to the Supreme Allied Commander South East Asia, Admiral Mountbatten.

It was Wedemeyer's belief that none other than Churchill himself was responsible in his reassignment to the CBI theatre because of his strongly sceptical views on the Mediterranean first strategy and that he was side-lined because of it.[77] This may

---

[75] Stoler, p. 109.
[76] Stoler, p. 115.
[77] Wedemeyer, p. 249.

have truth to it since it was Wedemeyer who, it has been assumed up until quite recently, had been charged directly by Marshall in 1941 to develop the *Victory Program* which was the initial US army services blueprint for the defeat of the Axis powers in Europe. At the heart of the *Victory Program* was the build -up of US forces in Britain in anticipation of a decisive cross channel assault in 1943. A strategy which Churchill and Brooke successfully pushed back on and thwarted over the next two years. Any doubts about Wedemeyer's antipathy towards the British and Roosevelt's policy of support is dispelled in his post-war memoir, *Wedemeyer Reports!,* whereby he heaps the ills of the Cold War upon the war time strategies of both Churchill and Roosevelt. Wedemeyer wrote in his opening chapter:

If we had followed the policy advocated by ex-president Hoover, Senator Taft, and other patriotic Americans, we probably would have stood aside until our intervention could enforce a just, and therefore enduring, peace instead of giving unconditional aid to Communist Russia. And if, after we became involved in the war, Roosevelt and Churchill had not sought to obliterate Germany, which was tantamount to destroying power equilibrium on the continent, we might not have fought in vain. [78]

Wedemeyer is an interesting character in the narrative of the wartime conferences and his twelve months under Mountbatten. There is a fundamental paradox to his avowed aversion to British strategic objectives during his time in Washington with the S&P Group and his loyal service to Mountbatten as his Chief of Staff. Wedemeyer represented the British sponsored Axiom mission to London and Washington in February 1944 to abandon the northern Burma operations (which included

---

[78] Wedemeyer, p. 3.

Operation Thursday) and pursue arguably more imperialistic objectives to the south, by invading the Andaman Islands and thereafter Malaya and Singapore. This was in direct opposition to Marshall's and Roosevelt's China strategy. Thereafter, upon replacing Stilwell in Chunking in late 1944, he reverted to opposing British policy versus the American position regarding Indochina. Recent research in the US now casts serious doubt on the importance of Wedemeyer to US planning and that much of the post –war appreciation of his input was his own fiction from his memoirs and subsequent interviews he gave.[79] Nevertheless the interregnum with Mountbatten is puzzling. In respect of the Chindits, Wedemeyer spoke often with Wingate during his time with SEAC and clearly held him in high regard.[80]

At the Symbol Conference at Casablanca the British were focused primarily on the continuation of the Mediterranean strategy with an attack on Sicily, with Husky now substituted in place of Brimstone. Marshall and the JCS grew increasingly impatient at British intransigence over Burma. On the first day of the conference Marshall had set out the strategic case for action in Burma as a means to reopen a land route that would get supplies to Chinese troops and General Chennault's bomber force operating in China. At a JCS meeting on the 17 January, prior to formal sessions with the CCS, Admiral King suggested that the Pacific situation should be discussed with the CCS at that morning's meeting when the JCS should insist that Operation Ravenous (the planned advance into northern Burma) be carried out and that Operation Anakim (the larger seaborne assault against Rangoon) be initiated not later than 1 November

---

[79] James Lacey, *Keep From All Thoughtful Men* (Annapolis, MD: Naval Institute Press, 2011).
[80] Wedemeyer, p. 251.

1943. King asserted that this operation was essential because of its importance to China and because the geographical position and manpower of China was the key to the defeat of Japan, just as the geographical position and manpower of Russia was the key to the defeat of Germany. Therefore, it was impossible to omit these operations from the JCS Pacific concept. Even if the question was not to be settled at this time, he felt it necessary to keep the British fully aware of the Pacific. King's thoughts are minuted as follows:

The British proposal to do nothing in Burma until the end of next year he characterized as fantastic. The diminishing prospect of being able to use any air bases in Russia was a further reason which compelled us to operate in Burma. [81]

Admiral King's comments at the JCS meeting on the 17 January underscore the emerging importance of Burma in American minds at this time as the key to securing a platform for striking back at Japan with strategic air resources. The failure of the 'Bradley Mission' at the end of December 1942 finally exhausted any hope that Stalin, prior to open hostilities between Russia and Japan, would entertain the idea of a long range bomber force being based on Russian territory to strike at industrial targets in Japan, or the US army units required to defend them.[82] In the event, such an opportunity would only

---

[81] CARL, Joint Chiefs of Staff Minutes Of Meeting Held at Anfa Camp on Sunday, 17 January 1943, at 0930hrs, *Casablanca Conference, January 1943, Papers & Minutes of Meetings 1943*.
<http://cgsc.contentdm.oclc.org/cdm/ref/collection/p4013coll8/id/3688> [accessed 29 March 2016]
[82] NARA, FDR Library, Map Room Papers, Box 25, JCS Report, The Bradley Mission, 27 December 1942, Conferences: Strategic Studies, Vol. 2, Prepared by JCS:

become viable when Russia declared war on Japan in the last weeks of the conflict by which time the US Pacific assault had transformed the offensive options open to the US. The conclusion that Russian offensive options were unlikely was circulated amongst the JCS in early January 1943 and informs Admiral King's comments regarding the lack of British efforts in Burma at the Symbol Conference a couple of weeks later. With the possibility of Siberian bases now firmly struck off the strategic options the JCS and American planners turned their eyes to China and Burma as a means to strike at Japan.[83]

The perceived reluctance of the British to take energetic action in Burma at this time also seemed at odds with intelligence reports in Washington to the JCS and CCS underlining the strategic importance of Burma to the Japanese economically, yet they were relatively weak militarily and posed minimal threat to the overall British position in India. An intelligence appreciation of Japanese economic capabilities in August 1942 further underscored the importance of the Allies regaining Burma, Malaya, Netherlands East Indies and the Philippines, in order to disrupt the Japanese access to critical

---

Japan-Torch Follow-Up, Franklin D. Roosevelt Library and Museum Website; version date 2016.

<http://www.fdrlibrary.marist.edu/_resources/images/mr/mr01 14.pdf> [accessed 8 March 2017]

[83] NARA, FDR Library, Map Room Papers, Box 25, Report to Joint Chief of Staff, JCS 182, 'Attacking Japan via the Northern Route – Siberia/ Kamchatka / Petropavlovsk', 5 January 1943, Conferences: Strategic Studies, II, Prepared by JCS: Japan-Torch Follow-Up, Franklin D. Roosevelt Library and Museum Website; version date 2016.
<http://www.fdrlibrary.marist.edu/_resources/images/mr/mr01 14.pdf> [accessed 8 March 2017]

resources. It also stressed the need to attack Japanese shipping carrying the raw materials and the need to concentrate air power against industrial targets in Manchuria.[84]Such targets would be in reach of airbases in Siberia or southern China. With the Russian option now firmly off the table it would have to be China, supplied via India and ideally northern Burma too, if only to neutralize the air threat from Japanese interception.

The threat assessment of the Japanese forces was also relatively low in Burma, assuming that the mounting of a major offensive was unlikely, save for a tactical opportunity to deny north east India to the Allied operations in support of China or against Burma. The most immediate and pressing threat in the American view was that Japan would neutralize Chiang Kai Shek via a separate peace deal, thus potentially releasing up to half a million IJA troops and air resources to the Pacific theatre.[85]

Allied intelligence reports in Washington at this time consistently played down the possibilities or scale of a Japanese

---

[84] NARA, FDR Library, Map Room Papers, Box 25, Memorandum for Information, No. 22, Joint US Combined Chiefs of Staff, 'Japanese Economic Capabilities', 31 August 1942, Conferences: Strategic Studies, II, Prepared by JCS: Japan-Torch Follow-Up, Franklin D. Roosevelt Library and Museum Website; version date 2016.
<http://www.fdrlibrary.marist.edu/_resources/images/mr/mr01 14.pdf> [accessed 8 March 2017]
[85] NARA, FDR Library, Map Room Papers, Box 25, Memorandum for Information, No. 25, Combined Chiefs of Staff, 'Japanese Intentions', 8 November 1942, Conferences: Strategic Studies, II, Prepared by JCS: Japan-Torch Follow-Up, Franklin D. Roosevelt Library and Museum Website; version date 2016.
<http://www.fdrlibrary.marist.edu/_resources/images/mr/mr01 14.pdf> [accessed 8 March 2017]

attack from Burma and focused on the greater strategic importance to the Japanese of their position in Melanesia.[86] With the Americans carrying the war to Japan in the Pacific there was a growing impatience for the British to do the same in Burma.

The British were not unaware of the strategic economic arguments for reoccupying Burma and were party to many of the same intelligence reports such as that analysing the Japanese fuel tanker resources and the importance of Burma and the Netherlands East Indies in providing, given time, for Japanese self -sufficiency in oil.[87] Such reports viewed in Washington pointed towards the need for both the denial of the oil fields and the destruction of Japanese shipping by air attack within range of the USAAF from bases in China.

General Wedemeyer offered that:

The British were firmly convinced that Germany would be defeated in 1943 and were, therefore, reluctant to take any resources away from the United Kingdom, in hopes that they

---

[86] NARA, FDR Library, Map Room Papers, Box 25, Report to Joint Intelligence Committee, No. 68, 'Japanese Capabilities in South East Asia in View of Commitments in Melanesia', 9 December 1942, Conferences: Strategic Studies, II, Prepared by JCS: Japan-Torch Follow-Up, Franklin D. Roosevelt Library and Museum Website; version date 2016. <http://www.fdrlibrary.marist.edu/_resources/images/mr/mr01 14.pdf> [accessed 8 March 2017]

[87] NARA, FDR Library, Map Rom Papers, Box 25, Joint Intelligence Committee, Report from London, 'The Japanese Tanker Position', 6 December 1942, shared with US 19 December 1942, Conferences: Strategic Studies, II, Prepared by JCS: Japan-Torch Follow-Up, Franklin D. Roosevelt Library and Museum Website; version date 2016. <http://www.fdrlibrary.marist.edu/_resources/images/mr/mr01 14.pdf> [accessed 8 March 2017]

would be able to conduct a successful cross- Channel operation. He personally felt it essential that Operation Ravenous should be done as soon as possible. The further they (the British) go with the operation, the less danger they will suffer from malaria when the rainy season starts. He felt it essential that the British be pressed to do everything they possibly could now.[88]

Operation Ravenous was a component in General Wavell's faltering plans for the re-conquest of Burma in late 1942 starting with limited operations in Akyab (Operation Cannibal) and then in the north across the Chindwin (Operation Ravenous) in which Wingate and the yet to be christened Chindits (77th Indian Brigade) were to be deployed in an experimental Long Range Penetration expedition, Operation Longcloth. Wavell wanted to do something, the British needed to demonstrate they were doing something, Wingate was keen to fight, so despite any other supporting action originally planned under Operation Ravenous, including a supporting role by Chinese forces, Longcloth alone went ahead. However, this was not simply a folly of Wingate, as is often described by his critics. It is vitally important to have an understanding of the context leading up to, and the agreement of operations, at Casablanca.

Marshall returned to the attack on the 17 January at the CCS session deploring the British recalcitrance over Ravenous and Anakim. When Brooke defended the British position based on a deficiency of naval support and landing craft, Admiral King and Rear Admiral Cooke stepped in and assured that the US

---

[88] CARL, Joint Chiefs of Staff Minutes of Meeting, JCS 53rd Meeting, Held at Anfa Camp on Sunday, 17 January 1943, at 0930hrs, *Casablanca Conference, January 1943, Papers & Minutes of Meetings 1943*.
<http://cgsc.contentdm.oclc.org/cdm/ref/collection/p4013coll8 /id/3688> [accessed 29 March 2016]

Pacific fleet would release sufficient resources to make up this deficiency. King saw Anakim as essential to the Allied strategy in defeating Japan by leveraging China's geographical position and potential manpower.[89] Marshall keen to impress further upon the British the need for an appreciation and awareness of a global strategy against the Axis reminded Brooke that, 'unless Anakim could be undertaken […] a situation might arise in the Pacific at any time that would necessitate the United States regretfully withdrawing from commitments in the European theatre.'[90]

Out of these tense and heated discussions came the agreed 1943 strategy for the CBI theatre as it related to the wider Pacific effort against the Japanese. The objectives and operations were laid out in the Symbol papers CCS 153-155, summarising the positions reached on 17- 18 January. The British acknowledged, 'tentatively', that Russia and Japan will remain non belligerent and that the Japanese need to be kept under continual pressure sufficient to erode the disposable Japanese resources. In Burma limited operations were to be conducted in the present dry season to improve lines of communications between India and China with more extended operations later in the year to re-establish communications along the lower Burma Road. This would have the effect of strengthening Chinese forces to keep China in the war, pressure the Japanese in this area, establish air strength to operate against

---

[89] Pogue, III, p. 25.

[90] CARL, C.C.S. 59th meeting, Minutes of Meeting held at Anfa Camp, on Sunday 17 January 1943, at 1030hrs, p. 228, *Casablanca Conference, January 1943, Papers & Minutes of Meetings 1943*.
<http://cgsc.contentdm.oclc.org/cdm/ref/collection/p4013coll8/id/3688> [accessed 29 March 2016]

enemy shipping in Chinese and Indochina ports.[91]In a redraft the British amended the assumptions to position Germany more clearly as the primary adversary to be defeated first and the objectives specifically as:

- To recapture and establish air forces at Akyab (Cannibal)
- To establish a bridgehead in the Chindwin Valley so that, when an attack on Rangoon is made, simultaneous pressure can be exerted on Mandalay (Ravenous)
- To construct the Hukawng Valley road from Ledo to Myitkyina and Lungling
- Detailed planning to reopen the Burma Road (Anakim) during the winter of 1943-44 will also be made.[92]

This British drafted paper submitted to the CCS on 17 January heavily caveated that the Anakim commitment in terms of the forces required, armed and naval, would react adversely on the early defeat of Germany.

A more detailed British paper was submitted the same day to

---

[91] CARL, Enclosure B, C.C.S. 153, 17 January 1943, Situation to be Created in the Eastern Theatre (Pacific and Burma) in 1943, *Casablanca Conference, January 1943, Papers & Minutes of Meetings 1943.*
<http://cgsc.contentdm.oclc.org/cdm/ref/collection/p4013coll8/id/3688> [accessed 29 March 2016]

[92] CARL, Memorandum by the British Joint Planning Staff, Situation to be Created in the Eastern Theatre (Pacific and Burma) in 1943, C.C.S. 153/1, 17 January 1943, *Casablanca Conference, January 1943*, Papers & Minutes of Meetings 1943.
<http://cgsc.contentdm.oclc.org/cdm/ref/collection/p4013coll8/id/3688> [accessed 29 March 2016]

further elaborate and caveat what British operations might be.[93] Geography dictated that only the trans-Burma route would deliver to China substantial supplies and that this necessitated the capture of Rangoon and Mandalay. The Japanese enjoyed the advantage of interior lines of communication and could therefore maintain greater forces in the Mandalay area than the British could from across the Assam frontier.

This British paper detailed specific operations that were already underway or planned; Wavell had launched Operation Cannibal to establish air forces at Akyab. Operation Ravenous, to be launched in February 1943, to establish IV Corps (two divisions) as a bridgehead in the Chindwin valley, in preparation for applying pressure on Mandalay when Rangoon was finally attacked. The British pointed out that the lines of communication from Assam could not support more than two divisions. This was to be completed in May 1943. In an acknowledgement of American wider strategic concerns, the British hoped that Ravenous would draw off some Japanese pressure from the Southwest Pacific. However, neither operation would reopen the land route to Burma, so the air transport route over the 'hump' remained the only immediate means of bringing relief to China. As for Anakim, the British could not see this as being possible before the winter of 1943-44 *at the earliest,* and required the recapture of both Rangoon and Moulmein, the latter to block enemy reinforcements from Thailand. The pressure by British forces in the Chindwin

---

[93] CARL, Report by the British Joint Planning Staff, Operations in Burma, 1943, C.C.S. 154, 17 January 1943, *Casablanca Conference, January 1943, Papers & Minutes of Meetings 1943.*
<http://cgsc.contentdm.oclc.org/cdm/ref/collection/p4013coll8/id/3688> [accessed 29 March 2016]

bridgehead would also be applied, and if possible by Chinese forces from Yunnan. The window of operations for Anakim was set out as 1 November 1943 – 30 April 1944. The main assault had to take place at the latest in early December 1943.

Again came the key and recurring British caveat at the end of the paper, 'If Operation Anakim is carried out with British assault shipping and landing craft at any time during the winter 1943-44, it would seriously curtail the British share of any cross-channel operations in the early spring of 1944.'[94]

The final agreed position paper was drawn up for agreement on 18 January, covering global strategy and the part in this that the CBI theatre played. The British had achieved everything they had really wanted strategically from the Symbol Conference at Casablanca; a renewed commitment to the Germany first approach, and only sufficient pressure on Japan to retain the initiative for full scale attack upon Germany's defeat. Subject to this, plans and preparations were to be made for the recapture of Burma (Anakim) beginning in 1943.[95]

The British also knew when putting these propositions forward that there was little prospect of an advance by Chinese forces from Yunnan. Chiang Kai Shek had already been clear that he would not commit Chinese forces without a British naval presence in the Bay of Bengal. As the British fleet was busy

---

[94] CARL, C.C.S. 154, p.15. *Casablanca Conference, January 1943, Papers & Minutes of Meetings 1943.*
<http://cgsc.contentdm.oclc.org/cdm/ref/collection/p4013coll8/id/3688> [accessed 29 March 2016]

[95] CARL, Memorandum by the Combined Chiefs of Staff, Conduct of the War in 1943, C.C.S. 155/1, 19 January 1943, *Casablanca Conference, January 1943, Papers & Minutes of Meetings 1943.*
<http://cgsc.contentdm.oclc.org/cdm/ref/collection/p4013coll8/id/3688> [accessed 29 March 2016]

securing the lines of communication off east Africa as a priority, this precondition was not going to materialize any time soon.

Mutual mistrust between the British and Chinese was an ever present factor that further complicated relationships between the British and the Americans. One didn't need to reach back to the previous century to draw inspiration for anti- British feelings, as recently as 1941 the British had closed the Burma Road to American aid to China, in the last desperate attempts to appease the Japanese prior to open hostilities. In mid - 1942 Wavell had only reluctantly accepted the remnants of Stilwell's Chinese force for training at Ramgarh, after they came out of Burma. He had not only security concerns about this Chinese force on Indian soil, but more practically and immediately, how to feed and equip such a force at the end of a long and tenuous line of communications? [96]

With the Allied forces retreating from Burma in disarray through April 1942, the British, Chinese and American alike, Chiang wrote to Roosevelt a detailed appreciation which amounted to a stinging criticism of the British armed forces and the lack of Allied air power. He requested this also be forwarded to Churchill.[97]

The Generalissimo was certainly persona non- grata by the British when he chose to meet the Indian National Congress leadership in July 1942. The exchange of memos between

---

[96] Victoria Schofield, *Wavell: Soldier and Statesman* (London: John Murray, 2006) p. 273.
[97] NARA, FDR Library, Map Room Papers, Box 10, Telegrams, Chiang Kai Shek to FDR, 13 April 1942, Exchange of Dispatches Between President Roosevelt and Generalissimo Chiang Kai Shek, 1941-42, Franklin D. Roosevelt Library and Museum Website; version date 2016. <http://www.fdrlibrary.marist.edu/_resources/images/mr/mr0059.pdf> [accessed 7 March 2017]

Chiang and Roosevelt at this time were deeply unsettling for Churchill and the Indian authorities. Chiang appealed to Roosevelt's anti-imperialist credentials in offering support for the INC and its hopes for an independent India and thereby securing Indian commitment to the war against Japan. Before responding and wary of the political minefield he was stepping into, Roosevelt shared Chiang's confidential memo with Churchill for an appreciation and advice on how to proceed.[98] Churchill's answer predictably dismissed Chiang's appreciation of the Indian situation and the importance of the INC. On the contrary, 'Their loyalty would be gravely impaired by handing over the government of India to Congress control.' Churchill concluded with, 'I earnestly hope therefore, Mister President, that you will do your best to dissuade Chiang Kai Shek from his completely misinformed activities, and will lend no countenance to putting pressure upon His Majesty's Government.'[99]

Roosevelt, taking Churchill's cues, acknowledged the Generalissimo's concerns over India but counselled that it was

---

[98] NARA, FDR Library, Map Room Papers, Box 10, Message for the President from the Generalissimo, 25 July 1942, Exchange of Dispatches Between President Roosevelt and Generalissimo Chiang Kai Shek, 1941-42, Franklin D. Roosevelt Library and Museum Website; version date 2016. <http://www.fdrlibrary.marist.edu/_resources/images/mr/mr00 59.pdf> [accessed 7 March 2017]

[99] NARA, FDR Library, Map Room Papers, Box 2, Cablegram 119 from London 30 July 1942, Churchill to FDR, received 31 July 1942, Churchill to FDR May – July 1942, II, Franklin D. Roosevelt Library and Museum Website; version date 2016. <http://www.fdrlibrary.marist.edu/_resources/images/mr/mr00 12a.pdf> [accessed 6 February 2017]

wiser not to undermine British authority there.[100]

Undeterred and emboldened by the arrests of Ghandi and Nehru, along with the rest of the INC Working Committee, Chiang appealed to Roosevelt to intervene, 'your Policy (on anti-imperialism) will serve as a guide to all of us who have resisted for so long and so bitterly the brute force of the aggressors.'[101] This can be read as both a rallying call to the South- East Asian peoples to have faith in Roosevelt's United Nation's declaration of 1941 regarding freedom and self-determination against the Japanese occupation, but of course also a lumping in of the British Empire too. This exchange of notes in mid – 1942 underscores the poisonous and mistrustful atmosphere between the 'Allies' in the CBI theatre with quite divergent interests and political objectives but with a common military foe, the Japanese.

Roosevelt, with his pretensions of anti-imperial crusading, which had far- reaching consequences for Indochina and

---

[100] NARA, FDR Library, Map Room Papers, Box 10, Message from the President to Chiang Kai Shek, 8 August 1942, Exchange of Dispatches Between President Roosevelt and Generalissimo Chiang Kai Shek, 1941-42, Franklin D. Roosevelt Library and Museum Website; version date 2016; Personal Message from President to Churchill, No. 176, Roosevelt to Churchill August – October 1942, Franklin D. Roosevelt Library and Museum Website; version date 2016. <http://www.fdrlibrary.marist.edu/_resources/images/mr/mr00 59.pdf> [accessed 7 March 2017]
[101] NARA, FDR Library, Map Room Papers, Box 10, Message from Chiang Kai Shek to Roosevelt, 11 August 1942, Exchange of Dispatches Between President Roosevelt and Generalissimo Chiang Kai Shek, 1941-42, Franklin D. Roosevelt Library and Museum Website; version date 2016. <http://www.fdrlibrary.marist.edu/_resources/images/mr/mr00 59.pdf> [accessed 7 March 2017]

America for the next forty years, was walking a political and diplomatic tightrope.[102] His response to Chiang is instructive as to the American challenge in cooperating with both the British and the Chinese in pursuing a primarily China agenda, through the agency of the only real military option, the British, with their own Imperial agenda, with China a most secondary consideration. Roosevelt advised Chiang that both the United States and China should only mediate if called upon to do so by both the British and the Congress Party. He reiterated the orders given to American forces in India:

The sole purpose of the American forces in India is to prosecute the war of the United Nations against the Axis powers. <u>In the prosecution of the war is that the primary aim of the Government of the United States is to aid China</u>. American forces in India will exercise scrupulous care to avoid the slightest participation in India's internal political problems, or even the appearance of so doing.[103]

---

[102] John J. Sbrega, 'Determination versus Drift: The Anglo-American Debate over the Trusteeship Issue, 1941-1945', *Pacific Historical Review,* 55/2 (May 1986), 256-280; 'The Anticolonial Policies of Franklin D. Roosevelt: A Reappraisal', *Political Science Quarterly*, 101 (1986), 65-84; '"First Catch Your Hare": Anglo –American Perspectives on Indochina during the Second World War', *Journal of South East Asian Studies*, 14/1 (March 1983), 63-78.

[103] NARA, FDR Library, Map Room Papers, Box 10, Message from Roosevelt to Chiang Kai Shek, 12 August 1942, Exchange of Dispatches Between President Roosevelt and Generalissimo Chiang Kai Shek, 1941-42, Franklin D. Roosevelt Library and Museum Website; version date 2016.

<http://www.fdrlibrary.marist.edu/_resources/images/mr/mr00 59.pdf> [accessed 7 March 2017]

The underlined sentence captures in 22 words the essence of the strategic tangle in the CBI Theatre between the three main Allies. Priorities were not just different by degrees, they diverged.

On the eve of the Casablanca conference in January 1943 it is therefore of no surprise that there remained a lack of a shared strategic view let alone cooperation between the British and the Chinese. An exchange of notes between Roosevelt, Chiang and Stillwell highlighted the refusal of Chiang to participate in Wavell's plans for a limited advance in northern Burma. Roosevelt impressed upon the Generalissimo the importance to China of reopening the Burma Road rather than the occupation of southern Burma (Anakim).[104] In reply, the Chinese leader gave his appreciation of the required strategy in Burma; that the Japanese had to be defeated on the Asiatic mainland rather than island hopping in the Pacific, hence the maximum effort in Burma was required. For Chiang, the British plans were simply insufficient, especially without the naval support and control of the Burmese coast, he believed Churchill had promised but was not forthcoming.[105] In true 'Vinegar Joe' style, Stilwell drafted

---

[104] NARA, FDR Library, Map Room Papers, Box 10, Memo from the President to Chiang Kai Shek, 2 January 1943, Exchange of Dispatches Between President Roosevelt and Generalissimo Chiang Kai Shek, 1943, Franklin D. Roosevelt Library and Museum Website; version date 2016. <http://www.fdrlibrary.marist.edu/_resources/images/mr/mr0060.pdf> [accessed 7 March 2017]

[105] NARA, FDR Library, Map Room Papers, Box 10, Memo from Chiang Kai Shek to the President via General Stilwell, 9 January 1943, Exchange of Dispatches Between President Roosevelt and Generalissimo Chiang Kai Shek, 1943, Franklin D. Roosevelt Library and Museum Website; version date 2016.

a scathing note, dripping with his legendary sarcasm as to Chiang's position on the operations and equally so, of the British:

I am unable to say definitely whether Chiang Kai Shek really expects to attack next fall, but I am sure that at that time the Japs will still fight, our supply lines will be bad, the Japs will have had more time to dig in, they will still be able to concentrate more quickly than we can, and we will still risk defeat. The British may or may not have an adequate force ready and they may or may not be able to put on a sea – borne attack, but if Chiang Kai Shek is to be the judge of British adequacy, he can still block action.[106]

The same appreciation was valid fifteen months later as Wingate prepared the fly- in for Operation Thursday, with one of his stated objectives being to encourage Chinese action from Yunnan, in northern Burma.

The timing of these cross currents is important regarding the build up to subsequent conferences in Washington and Quebec in 1943. The JCS had felt outmanoeuvred by the British over the Torch landings in November 1942 and positively misled over the cross channel invasion commitments earlier in the year. Going into the Symbol conference at Casablanca the JCS and its war planning staff were determined to provide a united US strategy versus the British preoccupation with the indirect

---

<http://www.fdrlibrary.marist.edu/_resources/images/mr/mr00 60.pdf> [accessed 7 March 2017]
[106] NARA, FDR Library, Map Room Papers, Box 10, Stilwell to Roosevelt, No. 30, 9 January 1943, Exchange of Dispatches Between President Roosevelt and Generalissimo Chiang Kai Shek, 1943, Franklin D. Roosevelt Library and Museum Website; version date 2016.
<http://www.fdrlibrary.marist.edu/_resources/images/mr/mr00 60.pdf> [accessed 7 March 2017]

approach in the Mediterranean. This led to the JCS threat to shift its priorities to the Pacific and brought Burma more sharply into their strategic focus. In the event, Roosevelt supported Churchill to pursue operations in Sicily and subsequently Italy, and reprimanded Marshall and the JCS over threats to switch to a Japan first global strategy. Chastised and professionally wounded, the JCS were determined to call the shots at Washington for the Trident talks in May 1943.

The Trident Conference at Washington

Churchill, in his post war recollections, records that regarding the India theatre he was, 'conscious of serious divergences beneath the surface which, if not adjusted, would lead to grave difficulties and feeble action during the rest of the year. I was resolved to have a conference at the highest possible level.'[107] How grave those difficulties might be required the British to summon the Indian Commanders in Chief; Field Marshall Wavell, Admiral Somerville, and Air Chief Marshall Peirse, in addition to the British Chiefs of Staff regular conference retinue. Churchill gives no hint in his memoirs of the drama between the senior British staff during the Atlantic voyage where much preparation was required for the coming two week conference with the JCS and Roosevelt in Washington. On the voyage Wavell was humiliated by Churchill and was only talked out of resigning there and then by the counsel of General Alan Brooke.[108] Churchill offered Wavell little comfort and was scathing in his summary of operations in Burma, in the preparation of his notes and opening positions for the forthcoming meeting with the Americans.

---

[107] Winston S. Churchill, *The Second World War*, 6 vols (London: The Folio Society, 2000), IV, p. 629.
[108] Alanbrooke, *War Diaries*, p. 400.

Wavell was convinced that Churchill had lost confidence in him, as he surely had, and no doubt as had others at the subsequent CCS staff meetings when Wavell provided a lengthy testimony as to the administrative, climatic, terrain and line of communication disadvantages preventing success in Burma. Wavell's gloomy account of his theatre of operations was delivered at the CCS meeting held at the White House on the 12 May 1943.[109] General Stilwell, who along with his 'Airpower' rival General Chennault, had also been recalled from the CBI theatre for the Trident talks, was probably expressing what many on the American side were thinking when he penned in his diary:

With Wavell in command, failure was inevitable; he had nothing to offer at any meeting except protestations that the thing was impossible, hopeless, impractical [...] After the Akyab fiasco, the four Jap divisions in Burma have them scared to death.[110]

As Wavell's biographer has recorded of the subsequent meetings on 14 May:

Wavell was quite at his worst, making the most heavy weather, in the most literal sense, about monsoons, floods and, finally mosquitoes [...] delivered in a dismal monologue with a deadpan face [...] American General Bill Somervell, who in withering tones said, 'and you suppose we don't have

---

[109] CARL, 1st Meeting at the White House, 2.30pm 12 May 1943, *Trident Conference, May 1943, Papers & Minutes of Meetings 1943* (Washington, DC: Office of the Combined Chiefs of Staff, 1943). <http://cgsc.contentdm.oclc.org/cdm/ref/collection/p4013coll8/id/3693> [accessed 29 March 2017]

[110] General Joseph W. Stilwell, *The Stilwell Papers: Iconoclastic Account of America's Adventures in China,* ed. by Theodore H. White (New York: De Capo, 1991), p. 205.

mosquitoes in the Pacific.'[111]

As the Trident Conference discussions evolved, Wavell continued to recount the British operations that had come to nought against great obstacles and challenges.[112] Amongst the three or four faltering projects under the British, Wavell related an account of operations in north Burma where a brigade was inserted from the IV Corps area across the Chindwin Valley to cover the Ledo Road operations and help the planned Chinese advance at the same time. When the Chinese took no supporting action Wavell had decided to deploy this Brigade anyway to gain experience of this form of fighting. Wavell was describing Operation Longcloth and the actions of Wingate's 77th Brigade, though this detail is not referenced in the official minutes. Wavell, having given a relatively detailed account of the actions of 77th Brigade deep behind Japanese lines summarised as follows, 'As a result of the experience gained, it had been decided to train one or possibly more brigades for this type of fighting.'[113] This entire narrative of Wavell's at Trident has only one positive note, the advance and operations of 77th Brigade, despite its privations and losses.

The subsequent conventional story regarding the Chindits has it that Wingate's report on Longcloth was suppressed or withheld until finally revealed to Churchill on the eve of the Quebec Conference in August, to which he was taken at short

---

[111] Schofield, p. 287.

[112] CARL, Item E, Operations in Burma, CCS 84th Meeting, 14 May, 10.30 AM 1943, *Trident Conference, May 1943, Papers & Minutes of Meetings 1943*.
<http://cgsc.contentdm.oclc.org/cdm/ref/collection/p4013coll8/id/3693> [accessed 29 March 2017]

[113] CARL, Item E, Operations in Burma, p. 353.
<http://cgsc.contentdm.oclc.org/cdm/ref/collection/p4013coll8/id/3693> [accessed 29 March 2017]

notice, almost on a whim by Churchill. This cannot be entirely true. The actions of 77th Brigade were known at Trident in mid-May 1943. The other conventional story is that though Wingate claimed that his report was suppressed this was not the case, it was more about official protocol and news management of a secret operation. Yet tantalisingly, in Forrest Pogue's personal notes, from his post war interviews with Marshall, is the comment that Marshall had fought for and insisted on the release of Wingate's Report. Pogue writes:

General Marshall developed a great fondness for Wingate. He said of him in 1956: 'Wingate was strong for me, because I printed over here his report on what was needed when the British staff suppressed it. I wouldn't go for that a damned bit. They didn't want him (down) here but I asked for him, and I pushed his project.' Of Wingate's talent he had no doubt: 'Wingate would have been in the class of Lawrence of Arabia but for his death.'[114]

This suggests that Wingate's Longcloth Report was indeed suppressed or only reluctantly released by the British, despite Churchill's patronage of Wingate.

At the subsequent Quadrant meetings at Quebec in August 1943, the utter contrast with Wavell's limp performance at the Trident meetings must have been a revelation to the JCS when Wingate was invited to confidently and expertly explain his ideas on Long Range Penetration in getting to grips with the Japanese in the jungles of Burma, without excuses, focused on the mission and the action required. From an American perspective that was when the Wingate myth was born and one in tune with their own ideas of how to shake the Burma theatre out of its lassitude and continual British excuses to avoid a land commitment in the north. Pogue summarises Wingate's impact

---

[114] Pogue, III, p. 257.

at Quebec thus, 'Wingate quickly won the backing of the American delegation for his proposals. Eager to get operations under way against the Japanese, General Marshall strongly supported the British officer's schemes.'[115]

To summarise the essence of the Allied positions regarding Burma from Casablanca through Trident to the Quadrant agreements; the Americans were consistent, the British were not. Burma mattered to the Americans for two key strategic reasons;

1. To support China and keep her in the war; in order to develop a firm base for Very Long Range bomber forces, which would open up the last phase of the war; the attrition of Japanese air resources, shipping and industry, and finally the assault proper on the Japanese home islands. This was much like the Pointblank operation in softening up Germany prior to the cross- channel assault.

China was of importance in its own right as a potential source of military manpower and the fact that anything from 500,000 – 750,000 Japanese military personnel were thought to be tied up in the occupation of China and Manchuria, as they were to be until the end of the war, despite the growing and ultimately decisive thrusts from the Pacific.

Burma was the important stepping stone to achieve this position in China, in securing the air link over the 'hump', better still to secure airfields in northern Burma, such as Myitkyina, in order to reduce the load over the high Himalayas and remove the Japanese air threat. Additionally, the clearing of northern Burma would be essential to the pushing through of the Ledo Road to reopen the land route to China and improve the tonnage in support of both Chiang's armies and the planned expansion of US air forces.

---

[115] Pogue, III, pp. 256-257.

2. To keep up the constant pressure against Japanese forces and wear them down in conjunction with, and to partly aid the Pacific operations of Nimitz and MacArthur. Operations in Burma would address that requirement.

None of these were addressing the real concerns of the British, who were primarily focused on Burma as simply an obstacle to the repossession of Malaya and Singapore, and only as a receding threat to the safety and security of India. At Casablanca, the British had committed to Anakim, the operation to invade Burma with amphibious landings in the south to secure Rangoon, which in itself would reopen the old Burma Road and avoid a wasteful slog across the northern valleys and mountains where superior weaponry could not be brought to bear. This was to commence in November 1943 with a series of preparatory operations on the coast to secure strategic position for air forces at Akyab and Ramree, and from the IV Corps area in the north to advance the road system to the Chindwin in readiness for Anakim.

The British came to Trident with Wavell's shockingly honest appreciation of how little had been achieved and could be achieved due to the administrative shortcomings of the lines of communication, the climate, the terrain, the health, training and low morale of British forces and above all the lack of shipping and naval resources. Anakim was not possible for another eighteen months, which meant an advance in 1945! Furthermore, the British averred that an advance into northern Burma was ill-advised for all the same reasons and the north could not be held anyway, even if an advance did succeed, because of the superior Japanese lines of communications.

The opening British offer at Trident was to back the air build up from Assam and focus all available resources on this single objective. The last point (8) in the British COS Memo from CCS 225 circulated for information on 14 May to the CCS could not have been less committed in meeting the requirements of their American allies:

The future of Anakim depends upon whether the re-conquest of Burma is found to be essential to the ultimate defeat of Japan. After the defeat of Germany we need a plan for the defeat of Japan, early and effective British participation depends on long-term preparations in India and Ceylon, which will be the basis of British operations, for which we need an agreed plan.[116]

The American position was set out in CCS 219 also circulated and read to the 84th Meeting of the CCS on 14 May by Admiral Leahy, Roosevelt's man on the US JCS committee, and Chairman of the JCS. This contained some uncomfortable messages for the British. Despite a continued commitment to the Germany first strategy, item 2(c) read, 'If however conditions develop which indicate that the war as a whole can be brought more quickly to a successful conclusion by the earlier mounting of a major offensive against Japan, the strategical concept set forth herein may be reversed.' Regarding operations in the Pacific and Far East, item 4(a) called for the maintenance of pressure on Japan, retain the initiative, contain the Japanese fleet in the Pacific, and attain or retain positions of readiness for a full scale offensive against Japan, and to keep China in the war. Item 4(c) detailed the offensive operations with the objectives of; firstly conducting air operations in and from China, secondly the seizure of Burma and thirdly, operations to secure the Aleutians, fourthly the Marshall and

---

[116] CARL, CCS 225, Operations from India, 1943-44, Circulated for Information, 14 May 1943, Memo from British Chiefs of Staff, *Trident Conference, Papers & Minutes of Meetings 1943.*
<http://cgsc.contentdm.oclc.org/cdm/ref/collection/p4013coll8/id/3693> [accessed 29 March 2017]

Caroline Islands, and fifthly the Solomons, the Bismarck Archipelago and New Guinea.[117]

In this strategy paper CCS 219, item 2(c), is the same threat, first raised in the arguments of 1942 prior to Torch, and again at Casablanca, for the Americans to refocus on the Pacific campaign. The Americans were well- prepared for the Trident Conference and were asserting their growing ascendancy in the Alliance. Such a threat could undermine the whole British strategy in Europe and the Mediterranean and any successful operations against Japan might in themselves create such a momentum.

Brower comments on this paper as follows:

Prepared by the American Joint Staff Planners (JSP) in the hectic days before Trident, CCS 219 was the hard line American view of how to conduct the war in 1943 and 1944 [...] As if casting down the gauntlet, the JCS presented the study to the British early in their meeting on May 14th.[118]

With such divergent goals regarding Burma a degree of compromise was required and this was mainly on the part of the British as the agreed strategy emerging out of Trident put them firmly on the hook for operations in Burma which completely disregarded their opening position. CCS 220, The Strategic Plan for the Defeat of Japan, was circulated at the 90th meeting of the CCS on 19 May and accepted as the basis for future combined study and elaboration of future plans. Point 2 (b) of this paper called for the maintenance and extension of unremitting

---

[117] CARL, CCS 219, Conduct of the War in 1943-44, Circulated 14 May, 84th CCS Meeting, *Trident Conference, Papers & Minutes of Meetings 1943*.
<http://cgsc.contentdm.oclc.org/cdm/ref/collection/p4013coll8/id/3693> [accessed 29 March 2017]

[118] Brower, pp. 27-28.

pressure on Japan to continually reduce her military power. The Plan itself was set out in six phases, the last being the invasion of Japan. Notably the first phase did not refer to the Pacific operations but focused on China and Burma as the foundation and entry point to develop and prosecute the war against Japan. Phase One of CCS 220 was set out to:

a) Continue and augment existing undertakings in and from China, with Chinese forces assisted by US forces.

b) Recapture Burma, with British forces assisted by US and Chinese forces.

c) Open the lines of communication to the Celebes Sea, with US forces.[119]

The final report that emerged from these requirements was set before Roosevelt and Churchill by the CCS on 25 May 1943, and was detailed in CCS 242/6.[120] As regards operations to defeat Japan in Burma a five stage strategy was laid out:

1. Concentration of available resources as first priority in Assam / Burma to attain 10,000 tons per month in air supply to China, intensifying air operation against Japan in Burma, maintaining increased AAF in China, maintaining the flow of airborne supplies to China.

---

[119] CARL, CCS 220, Conduct of the War in 1943-44, 20 May 1943, *Trident Conference, Papers & Minutes of Meetings 1943*.
<http://cgsc.contentdm.oclc.org/cdm/ref/collection/p4013coll8/id/3693> [accessed 29 March 2017]

[120] CARL, CCS 242/6, Final Revision, Final Report to the President and Prime Minister, Memo by the CCS, 25 May 1943, *Trident Conference, Papers & Minutes of Meetings 1943*.
<http://cgsc.contentdm.oclc.org/cdm/ref/collection/p4013coll8/id/3693> [accessed 29 March 2017]

2. Vigorous and aggressive land and air operations at the end of the 1943 monsoon from Assam into Burma via Ledo and Imphal, in step with a Chinese advance from Yunnan – with the objective of containing as many Japanese forces as possible, covering the air route to China and as an essential step towards opening the Burma Road.

3. Capture of Akyab & Ramree Islands by amphibious operations.

4. Interruption of Japanese seas communications into Burma.

5. Continuance of the administrative preparations in India for eventual launching of an overseas operation of about the size of Anakim.

Thus, the British had got the focus on the air resource build up in Assam and the effective cancellation of operations to recapture Burma, but they had to conduct significant ground and air operations in Burma to support the US objectives in China and the US concept of a strategy for the defeat of Japan. The continued resistance to such ground operations by the British were summarised earlier by General Brooke at the 90th Meeting of the CCS on 20 May, regarding Item 4, Operations In Burma to Open and Secure an Overland Route to China, 'The British Chiefs of Staff believed there was a great danger in extensive operations from Ledo and Imphal, depending on two very precarious roads whereas the Japanese would be supplied by road, rail and rivers, and would be operating out of a relatively dry area.'[121] At the same meeting Wavell proposed the use of

---

[121] CARL Minutes, 90th Meeting of CCS, 20 May 1943 10.30am, CCS 231, Item 4, Operations in Burma to Secure an Overland Route to China, *Trident Conference, Papers & Minutes of Meetings 1943.*
<http://cgsc.contentdm.oclc.org/cdm/ref/collection/p4013coll8/id/3693> [accessed 29 March 2017]

LRP brigades in northern Burma to maintain contact between the British and Chinese forces. Marshall in summing up at this meeting acknowledged the British reservations but could not conceive of a build- up of the air operations not producing a strong Japanese reaction, so there must be ground operations too.

So at Trident we can see the threads of strategy and available resources coalescing into the agreements to be made at Quebec. The British were again required to commit to operations in northern Burma much against their better judgement. The only positive aspect of operations since Casablanca were in northern Burma with Operation Longcloth and 77th Brigade, despite its negligible military achievements. Going into the Quebec Conference the British needed a solution for fighting in northern Burma to placate US strategic requirements and Wingate was that ready solution.

The evolution of the Allied positions in the various conferences prior to Quebec in August 1943 set out above bust the myth that Wingate was opportunistically thrust onto centre stage simply on a whim by Churchill on the eve of the First Quadrant Conference. Planning and reforming of LRP brigades was already taking place at Wavell's instruction and he saw them as being a key part of addressing US requirements of the British in northern Burma. So too did Churchill and Marshall.

By the time of the Quebec Conference the continued recalcitrant British attitude to the Trident Agreement saw Churchill and his Chiefs of Staff needing Wingate and his LRP tactics to offer a plausible British response on the part of the British to the strategic wishes of the US. It is no surprise that Marshall had admiration for Wingate, an Englishman who was palpably not afraid of engaging the Japanese in the jungles of northern Burma. Wavell, the main British advocate of Wingate, at the head of the Indian Army, was unfortunately for Wingate,

no longer in charge of British forces by the time of the Quebec
Agreement.

Chapter Three: Operation Longcloth &
the Quadrant Conference at Quebec

'Am I to be court martialled or commended?'[122]

The conventional narratives of Operation Longcloth tend to dwell on its perceived lack of military results and high cost in casualties. The fact that up to a third of Wingate's force was lost and many more left unfit for further duty is often the leading and most salient point made. The direct military achievements were indeed slight despite the unquestioned bravery and daring of most of the columns, especially Calvert's. For the staunch anti – Wingate writers, this is the sum total of the achievements of Longcloth, which was then distorted by Wingate's opportunism and Churchill's adulation and weakness for a romantic warrior figure, symbolic of Britain's sleeping military potential. For those narratives that are a little less grudging in their assessment of Wingate, there is a recognition that Longcloth did demonstrate a new bold and offensive spirit in British troops, something that had been so conspicuously lacking in 1942 and it did raise morale and present a better martial image, both at home and abroad.

Louis Allen, in his comprehensive and balanced account of the campaign, *Burma: The Longest War,* probably captures the appropriate mood in describing Wingate's first operation:

LONGCLOTH had panache, it had glamour, it had cheek, it

---

[122] TNA, CAB 106/206, Slim's comments on Wingate's reported first words on re-entering India after Longcloth, Notes on Meeting with Field Marshall Slim, Interview notes by Lt. Col. J.E.B. Barton, 1. Comments on First Chindit Expedition, Narrative on Operations of Special Force.

had everything the successive Arakan failures lacked. It was the perfect psychological medicine for an Army sadly devoid of confidence in its methods, its purposes and its ability to fulfil them.[123]

It was certainly not just business as usual on the Burma Front. Wingate's post -operation report on Longcloth has an unashamed tone of self -confidence and can- do attitude. The difficulties of weather, terrain, supply, communications and the enemy are merely described as obstacles to overcome.[124] How this must have jarred with the prevailing image and reports to the American Allies as to why any meaningful offensive action by the British was impossible in Burma. In particular, Wavell's rather downbeat and pessimistic assessment of current operations and prospects at the Washington Conference with the CCS in May would seem as day and night with that of Wingate's Report.[125] Here was a potential blue print from Wingate on how to get to grips with the Japanese in Burma.

As has already been identified, the idea of using Wingate's forces and concept of LRPGs was already in currency amongst the CCS at the Trident Conference in May 1943, three months before Quadrant. It is a misconception, or worse, a part of the

---

[123] Louis Allen, *Burma: The Longest War, 1941-45* (London: J.M Dent, 1984; repr. 1986), p. 118.

[124] Brigadier Orde C. Wingate, *Report on Operations of 77th Indian Infantry Brigade in Burma February –June 1943* (New Delhi: Government of India Press, 1943).

[125] CARL, Combined Chiefs of Staff, Trident Revised Minutes 2nd meeting, The White House, 2:00 p.m., 14 May 1943, *Trident Conference, Papers & Minutes of Meetings 1943* (Washington, DC: Office of the Combined Chiefs of Staff, 1943).
<http://cgsc.contentdm.oclc.org/cdm/ref/collection/p4013coll8/id/3693> [accessed 29 March 2017]

anti-Wingate myth, that the idea to use LRPGs extensively was a spur of the moment idea of Churchill's. The idea was in fact Wavell's, who was the senior sponsor of Wingate in bringing him to Burma in 1942, being aware of his methods and capabilities as GOC in the Middle East and in particular of Wingate's successes with Gideon Force in Ethiopia the previous year. It was Wavell, who prior to his promotion-cum-removal to Governor General of India, had already taken the decision to expand Wingate's force following Operation Longcloth. It was Wingate's misfortune, despite the most powerful political and military backing at Quebec in August 1943, that with Wavell already gone, so was Wingate's political support, in India at least, from the resentment and obstruction of the Indian Army establishment.

Slim's post war reflections on Operation Longcloth are no less harsh than those he made of Operation Thursday, the following year. Interviewed in 1953, as part of the research for the *Official History,* his impression was 'one of rather wasted effort.' In the interview, Slim goes on to diminish other aspects of the mission:

We learnt little new in the way of air supply, which we had already tested and nothing of air transportation of troops. The great value of the expedition in his opinion was its effect on morale of other troops – and the man mainly responsible for this was F.M. Wavell, who, on Wingate's return to India, staged a press day at HQ 4 Corps, Imphal, and on the B.B.C. It was a "phoney" morale, in that what was claimed for the expedition was palpably untrue, e.g. that they had defeated the Japs at their own game, inflicted enormous damage to their communications, inflicted casualties, upset their strategic plans and so on [...] But it had the great merit of diverting public attention from the failure in the Arakan and of bringing the expedition to the notice of the Americans – and incidentally of

Winston Churchill too. Its chief practical value was the use F.M. Slim and other commanders in Burma made of it to point out if one lot could beat Japs in the jungle so could the rest.[126]

Slim's comments in this interview with Lt. Col. Barton in 1953 are perhaps a little too ingenuous, with the hindsight of the ultimate Burma victory behind him and his own reputation still in the ascendancy; *Defeat into Victory* was still three years away. At the time of Longcloth, February to May 1943, the Arakan debacle was just yet another in the continuing sequence of reverses that put the reputation of British forces at rock bottom in the eyes of the British, from Churchill down to the general public, the American military and of course, the Japanese. There can be no doubt that Wingate not only chose to take his expedition forward when all hope of British and Chinese support had melted away, he actually insisted to Wavell it was the right thing to do if the British were ever to get on the front foot in Burma.

Wavell, for his part, did carefully choreograph the story of Longcloth for the media but what military commander in charge of a theatre didn't? Of course a positive appreciation and exploitation was put on the mission and its aftermath, and it had the desired effect. National newspapers in May 1943 carried headlines such as, 'British Jungle Force Kept Japanese on the Run,'[127] and 'Commando in the Jungle, Raids into Burma,' [128] and 'Wingate Wrecking Expedition in Burma.' [129] The press

---

[126] TNA, CAB 106/206, Slim, Comments to Barton on the Narrative on Operations of Special Force, 2 April 1953.

[127] Marsland L. Gander, 'British Jungle Force Kept Japanese on the Run', *Daily Telegraph*, 21 May 1943.

[128] Special Correspondent, 'Commando in the Jungle, Raids into Burma', *Times,* 21 May 1943.

[129] Special Correspondent, 'Wingate Wrecking Expedition in Burma', *Times*, 24 May 1943.

stories made the most of a modest raid and were part of the catalyst that revived interest and confidence in the theatre. It should also be borne in mind that at the time of these managed stories in the press Wavell was fighting for his own military reputation and career in Washington at the Trident meetings. Wavell had even felt compelled to seriously consider his resignation, due to Churchill's obvious and unconcealed loss of confidence in him during the pre -conference preparations on the Atlantic crossing to Washington.[130]

Two of the well-known Chindit Officers from the Longcloth expedition, Major J.B. Jeffries and Squadron Leader R.G.K. Thompson, were heavily publicised by the military authorities and were flown back to the UK in June 1943 to conduct a series of press interviews and public engagements.[131] The Times reported on 30 June:

Two members of the expedition which Brigadier O.C. Wingate led into the mountain fastness of Northern Burma a few months ago have arrived in Britain to tell their own story of an intrepid operation in which ordinary British and Gurkha troops proved conclusively that, given the proper training, they are able to master the Japanese in the jungle.[132]

Jeffries and Thompson also met with CIGS, Sir Alan Brooke, who found them, 'very interesting.'[133] This propaganda and publicity tour was expanded to include an extensive itinerary of the United States which overlapped with the Quadrant Conference in Quebec. While in New York they gave a series

---

[130] Alanbrooke, *War Diaries*, p. 400.

[131] Sir Robert Thompson, KBE, *Make for the Hills* (London: Pen & Sword, 1989), pp. 35-40.

[132] Special Correspondent, 'Mastery in the Jungle', *Times*, 30 June 1943.

[133] Alanbrooke, *War Diaries*, p. 425.

of interviews to journalist Charles Rolo, who published an adulatory account of the Chindit Expeditions in 1944.[134] Thompson and Jeffries finally reported back for duty in India in October 1943.

The extent of the promotion of the Chindits' exploits on the Longcloth mission, as evidenced in the tour outlined above, which covered multiple public meetings far and wide across the United States, together with Wavell's management of the news from India HQ and his decision to raise a second Chindit force, positioned for future operations at the Washington Conference in May, surely negates the myth that Wingate's ascendancy was simply a flight of Churchill's fancy. Sir Alan Brooke too, had interviewed and debriefed Wingate on his return to London and also supported the raising of a larger Chindit force as a means of getting to grips with the Japanese in Burma. It is notable what Sir Alan Brooke records in his post diary additions to his record of this meeting, prior to the journey for Quadrant, *and* prior to Wingate's elevation in the meetings with the Americans, 'I provided him with all the contacts in England to obtain what he wanted, and told him that on my return from Canada I would go into the whole matter with him to see that he had obtained what he wanted.' [135] Wingate must already have been a key part of British plans in Burma prior to Quadrant with the clear backing of the CIGS himself. This was not just a fancy of Churchill's. Sir Alan Brooke was very much his own man who shot down or contained many of Churchill's more unsound ideas and was therefore unlikely to be simply reacting to Winston's latest military conceit.

---

[134] Charles J. Rolo, *Wingate's Raiders: an Account of the Fabulous Adventure That Raised the Curtain on the Battle for Burma* (London: George G. Harrap, 1944).
[135] Alanbrooke, *War Diaries*, p. 436.

Brigadier Ferguson, one of the key figures in the Chindit leadership had the following observations on Longcloth, soon after the end of the war:

The achievement of that first expedition was not spectacular but it provided useful experience. We learned a great deal about tactics, about the shortcomings (as well as the virtues) of the Japanese as a fighting man, about the military topography of the country, and about the enemy's communication system. We also proved that supply-dropping was feasible. On the credit side also we had some considerable damage to the Mandalay-Myitkyina railway; a number of dead Japanese; and the fact that we had put them off their stroke, and caused them to call off more than one projected operation.[136]

Slim's comments on the lack of anything innovative being contributed to air supply operations during Longcloth is not supported by the *Official History*:

By far the most valuable lesson learnt was that forces could be maintained in jungle country by air supply, demanded by wireless as and when required. Provided air superiority could be retained and sufficient transport aircraft made available, an offensive into Burma across the grain of the country was no longer of necessity tied to roads which could only be built slowly and with great difficulty. Given these two conditions, commanders were to find themselves once again with strategical and tactical freedom. Thus, even if the enterprise had little or no strategical value, it was worth the effort expended.[137]

From a Japanese perspective the impact of Longcloth, though relatively minor militarily, appears to be not as slight and ineffectual as Slim asserts. It did have strategic consequences

---

[136] Brig. Bernard Fergusson, 'Upper Burma, 1943-44', *The Geographical Journal*, 107/1/2 (January-Feb. 1946), 1-10.
[137] Kirby, II, p. 327.

according to post war interrogations of Japanese officers by the US military:

At the end of May, all of the Wingate force had been driven west of the Chindwin River. Mopping-up operations in the vast jungle zone were extremely difficult and exhausted the troops and, since such operations had not been anticipated, units lacked the necessary equipment, training and supplies. In addition, units often suffered heavy losses from enemy light automatic weapons in jungle ambuscades. The exhaustion of the men due to inadequate supplies was serious and the Army's plan for restoration of fighting potential and the retraining of troops had to be abandoned.[138]

The *Japanese Monograph 134* further stated:

As a result of the Wingate Operations, the 15th Army, which had established comparatively simple defences, realized that during the dry season the movement of pack horse units in the jungle of northern Burma was unrestricted in many places and that it was easy to cross the Chindwin River by using locally obtainable materials for rafts. The Army had estimated that a counterattack by large enemy groups would be impossible without first repairing the roads and that it would be possible to check small enemy counteroffensives indefinitely if the existing roads and trails leading to India were strongly defended. However, this reasoning was now changed and the change prompted a thorough investigation of the defensive measures employed in central and northern Burma. It was feared that

---

[138] CARL, *Japanese Monograph 134, Burma Operations Record, 15th Army Operations in Imphal Area and Withdrawal to Northern Burma, Revised Edition* (Tokyo: Headquarters United States Army, Japan, 1952; revised 1957), p. 8.
<http://cgsc.contentdm.oclc.org/cdm/ref/collection/p4013coll8/id/2605> [accessed 29 march 2016]

present defences would collapse if such counterattacks were to be repeated by several echelons of the enemy.[139]

We should also recall the fact that the *Official History* by Kirby made light of this Japanese testimony, as was pointed out by Mead.[140] It is worth quoting at length from this *Japanese Monograph 134*, if only to counter - balance the official and authoritative voices of Slim and Kirby. This Japanese testimony categorically refutes Slim's assertion that it was 'palpably untrue' that the Japanese strategic plans had been upset. The Japanese specifically detail the reorganisation of the 15th Army, the reassessment of its strategic intent regarding India, and the upset of its plans as a direct or associated result of the Wingate raid! Having rejected the initial plans for the invasion of India, Japanese Operational Plan No. 21, General Mutaguchi was directly influenced by Wingate, and *Monograph 134* continues as follows:

The 15th Army was driven by necessity to give up its original defence plan and advance the first defence line from the Zibyu Range west to the Chindwin River. Realizing that the Chindwin River would not serve as a major obstacle during the dry season the Army staff then considered it necessary to advance the first defence line further west to the steep Arakan Range and to launch an offensive into India, the source of enemy operations. The Army commander believed that preparations for an invasion of India could be conducted without difficulty because there still remained considerable time before the next dry season. He believed that a bold strike at Assam would be best,

---

[139] CARL, *Japanese Monograph 134*, pp. 9-10.
<http://cgsc.contentdm.oclc.org/cdm/ref/collection/p4013coll8/id/2605> [accessed 29 march 2016]
[140] Peter Mead, *Orde Wingate and the Historians* (Braunton: Merlin, 1987), p. 153.

as such an operation would deal a severe blow to the British by destroying their counteroffensive bases in India and would ultimately result in fomenting the struggle for Indian Independence.[141]

The monograph continues:

General Mutaguchi, 15th Army Commander, had not abandoned his plan to invade eastern India, however, the Army did not have authority to operate across the Burma-India border. He determined, therefore, to carry out the operation of re-establishing the line as the initial step toward the eventual execution of his plan for the invasion of eastern India. The movement to the west was termed the "Bu"Operation.[142]

Furthermore:

Owing to the exigencies of the Akyab and Wingate Operations few 33rd Division units were allowed the periods of rest or training that had been expected. After the pursuit of Wingate, the division was forced to secure the strategic area along the Chindwin River and emphasis was placed on positive operations.[143]

If this Japanese testimony in *Monograph 134* is to be relied upon it clearly asserts that Wingate's first expedition did directly affect Japanese strategic thinking and military plans and was more than a mere nuisance. For the first time in the

---

[141] CARL, *Japanese Monograph 134*, p. 18.

<http://cgsc.contentdm.oclc.org/cdm/ref/collection/p4013coll8/id/2605> [accessed 29 march 2016]

[142] CARL, *Japanese Monograph 134*, p. 20.
<http://cgsc.contentdm.oclc.org/cdm/ref/collection/p4013coll8/id/2605> [accessed 29 march 2016]

[143] CARL, *Japanese Monograph 134*, p. 22.
<http://cgsc.contentdm.oclc.org/cdm/ref/collection/p4013coll8/id/2605> [accessed 29 march 2016]

Burma theatre we might describe the British, through Wingate's efforts, of imposing their will on the Japanese, presenting them with a new problem and impacting (ultimately disastrously at Kohima and Imphal) on the Japanese defence of Burma. This is one of the key points of Liddell Hart's assessment of successful strategy, 'Whatever the form, the effect to be sought is the dislocation of the opponents mind and dispositions – such an effect is the true gauge of an indirect approach.'[144] Wingate imposed his will on Mutaguchi by altering both his and the Imperial Japanese Burma Army strategy west of the Chindwin. In the subsequent Operation Thursday in March 1944, Wingate pinned Mutaguchi's attention to Chindit operations from his Army HQ in Maymyo for a crucial two months, rather than directing operations from his advance HQ across the Chindwin, 200 miles further west.

This Japanese account of the impact of Longcloth is partially accepted by the *Official History* which in its concluding paragraph on the chapter, "The First Chindit Operation", asseses that, 'The incursion into Burma by the Chindits was thus instrumental in bringing about a change in Japanese military thinking and led them to adopt a new policy in Burma. This was the outstanding outcome of the operation.'[145]

In January 1946, Major General G.W. Symes, GOC 70th Indian Division, which had been broken up to largely create the Special Force required by the Quadrant decisions, but who loyally served as Wingate's second in command, interrogated three Japanese officers to garner their views on the impact of

---

[144] Basil Liddell Hart, *Strategy* (London: Faber & Faber, 1954; repr. 1991) p. 147.
[145] Kirby, II, p. 329.

the Chindit operations of 1943 and 1944.[146] Regarding Longcloth, this reflected other Japanese testimonies as to the lack of any real military results or lasting damage, with the railway and bridges destroyed being repaired within a month.[147] It does, however, identify two specific results of Longcloth; firstly a newly created hostility towards the Japanese on the part of the Burmese villagers, and secondly a change in Japanese strategic thinking and plans regarding offensive operations against the British in India.

This interrogation report of Symes's was independent and pre- dates the *Japanese Monograph 134*, translated from the Japanese original by the Americans in 1952. The three Japanese officers interrogated by Symes, Lt. General Kimura, Burma Area Army Command, Lt. General Naka, Chief of Staff, Burma Area Army Command and Major Kaetsu, G.S. (Ops) Burma Area Army Command, were not listed amongst the 23 officers named in the *Japanese Monograph 134*.[148] This report by Symes independently corroborates the views of the Japanese in *Monograph 134* and also provides additional evidence on the impact of Longcloth. If the operation had helped rekindle the fighting spirit of the British it had a similar effect on the Burmese in the area of operations.

The interrogation reports that, 'Prior to this (Longcloth), the inhabitants of the area of operations were friendly to, and

---

[146] TNA, WO 106/4827, Maj. General Symes, Japanese Views on the Wingate Expeditions of 1943 and 1944, 27 January 1946.

[147] CARL, *Japanese Monograph 134*, p. 21
<http://cgsc.contentdm.oclc.org/cdm/ref/collection/p4013coll8/id/2605> [accessed 29 march 2016]

[148] CARL, *Japanese Monograph 134*, pp. iii-iv.
<http://cgsc.contentdm.oclc.org/cdm/ref/collection/p4013coll8/id/2605> [accessed 29 march 2016]

cooperative with, the Japs. Afterwards, they became unfriendly and non –co-operative.'[149] It is interesting to note that this effect accords with one of Wingate's objectives for Long Range Penetration missions and is also reflected in the memoirs of leading Chindits like Bernard Ferguson as to the intended impact on the Burmese of an audacious British presence behind Japanese lines. Regarding the impact on the strategic designs of the Japanese the interrogation report continues:

At that time, 18 Div. were training for an operation planned for early 1944, i.e. an advance from Myitkyina northwards into Assam, and directed on Tinsukia. The Wingate expedition changed this. It showed them that if the British could come from the East across the Chindwin, they likewise could go Westwards against Imphal and Kohima. The Tinsukia plan was accordingly scrapped.[150]

Symes's assessment on the veracity of the Japanese answers given in the interrogation was, 'In the main, I consider the information given to be correct.'[151]

During the Quadrant sessions at Quebec, General Auchinleck, as Commander in Chief India, issued a grudging cover note on 18 August 1943 to Wingate's Longcloth Report[152], whereby he cautioned on the proper usage of LRPG's as part of a larger conventional force, berated some of Wingate's more intemperate remarks and summarised five positive

---

[149] TNA, WO 106/4827, Symes, p. 2.

[150] TNA, WO 106/4827, Symes, p. 2.

[151] TNA, WO 106/4827, Symes, p. 1.

[152] Brigadier Orde C. Wingate, *Report on Operations of 77th Indian Infantry Brigade in Burma February –June 1943* (New Delhi: Government of India Press, 1943); note that this is the original report that Auchinleck is referring to, and not the plan put before the CCS and developed with the British COS at the Quadrant Conference.

achievements of Longcloth. These were the ability of the British to re-enter Burma and the inability of the Japanese to stop them, the temporary destruction of the Mandalay – Myitkyina railway and disruption to Japanese lines of communication, the drawing off of six to eight battalions to deal with the raid, the collection of valuable information on the topography and conditions in occupied Burma and the good moral effect on our own troops generally and on the public, both in India and abroad.[153]

This note of Auchinleck's is curious as it is addressing the Wingate Report of June 1943, which is actually fully titled, *Report to Commander 4th Corps on Operations of 77th Indian Infantry Brigade in Burma February to May 1943*. One assumes therefore, that Auchinleck upon receiving demands from the British COS direct from Quadrant on the raising of six or more LRPG's, hasn't actually seen the subsequent Quadrant report to the US JCS written by Wingate together with the British COS during the sea voyage to Canada in early August. Auchinleck's opening comment is a study in understated restraint on his true feelings on the matter, 'I wish to emphasize that this report is the report of the Commander 77 Indian Infantry Brigade to the Commander 4 Corps. It contains opinions with which I am not necessarily in full agreement.'[154]

The series of messages that flowed to and fro between India and Quebec at this time, that ultimately led to the break -up of General Symes's 70th Division, in order to create the required LRPG's must be the motive for this note of Auchinleck's dated 18 August. Under the paragraph titled 'Functions of Long Range Penetration Groups', we see a foreshadowing of the arguments and conclusions of Slim and Kirby a dozen or more

---

[153] TNA, AIR 23/1944, Auchinleck, H.E. The C-in-C India, Notes on First Wingate Expedition, 1943, 18 August 1943.
[154] TNA, AIR 23/1944, Auchinleck, paragraph 1.

years later:

Long Range Penetration Groups must be considered in their proper perspective [...] They are of value if they contain superior forces away from the main effort, or if their operations, offensive or destructive, have an effect on the enemy's conduct of the main battle [...] their commanders must direct and subordinate their actions to the achievement of success by the main effort.

This next excerpt is hardly different from what Slim wrote in *Defeat into Victory*:

To use Long Range Penetration Groups alone and unsupported is unlikely to achieve results commensurate with the almost certain loss of a large proportion of these highly trained and specialised troops.[155]

Prior to this note from Auchinleck though, is a summary report of Longcloth titled 'Lessons from Longcloth', dated 30 July to Eastern Army HQ and signed by Lt. General Scoones, Commander of IV Corps under whose overall operational control 77th Brigade and Wingate were placed.[156] A more detailed report is attached to this, '4 Corps, Longcloth Lessons'. This document must have been primarily written by General Scoones as it has numerous comments regarding shortcomings of the Longcloth operation and also of Wingate. The Wingate Report itself was cleared chapter by chapter as it was written by Wingate via General Scoones in the period of its writing mid – May to mid –June 1943. In Scoones's report, the recommendation for the raising of 6 LRPG's is accepted. The paragraph closes, 'Let us make sure that we utilise our

---

[155] TNA, AIR 23/1944, Auchinkleck, Functions of Long Range Penetration Groups.
[156] TNA, AIR 23/1944, Lt. Gen. Scoones, Lessons from Longcloth, 30 July 1943.

advantage to the full and do not skimp the LRPG's in any way, number of groups, equipment or high grade personnel.'[157] The words may be Wingate's from his original report but the endorsement is Scoones's and IV Corps. This paragraph is actually summarised for the leading lesson highlighted in Scoones's summary page at the front of the report:

Future employment – The operations proved that Long Range Penetration Groups (L.R.P.G.) of the LONGCLOTH type will assist materially towards the successful conclusion of operations in Burma, if employed in direct co-operation with the main force. Six L.R.P.G.'s should be formed.[158]

In addition to the future employment of LRPG's the summary report goes on to highlight key lessons on personnel, 'High quality troops must be employed. Both officers and men should be hand -picked.'[159]

Further comments are made, far from uncritical, on training, command, control, air co-operation, supply dropping and communications. Scoones's report generally gives a full endorsement to the LRPG concept and the raising of six brigades for future use but that the force must operate within the framework and command of IV Corps. In the introduction his detailed report on '4 Corps Longcloth Lessons', setting out this point of view, he opens with; 'The great majority of the lessons learned from LONGCLOTH have been dealt with in Brigadier WINGATE's report and I am in general agreement with the

---

[157] TNA, AIR 23/1944, Scoones, Lessons from Longcloth, p.2. [Note that only the introduction includes pagination.]

[158] TNA, AIR 23/1944, Scoones, Lessons from Longcloth, Future Employment.

[159] TNA, AIR 23/1944, Scoones, Lessons from Longcloth, Personnel.

views he expressed in it.'[160] Regarding Wingate himself, Scoones made the following comment:

...in spite of the many adverse factors with which Brig. Wingate had to compete, the most serious of these being the quality of the majority of the personnel which he was given and the lack of training of a large number who only joined at the last moment. This success under these conditions only serves to emphasise the remarkable qualities of leadership displayed by Brig. Wingate.[161]

It is worth recapping on the Wingate myth regarding Quebec at this point. Far from being simply a flight of fancy of Churchill's in taking Wingate to Quebec after dining with him in London, it is clear that Wingate is accepted as an important part of future British operations in Burma. Longcloth and its lessons weren't just a PR stunt that got out of control, it was a part of the emerging plan for getting to grips with the Japanese. Wavell acknowledge this in his submissions to the CCS at Trident in May, Sir Alan Brooke acknowledged this in his diary entry in July after debriefing Wingate, prior to Churchill's dinner with Wingate on the eve of sailing to Quebec. That Churchill chose to promote the idea of Wingate and the Chindits as part of his theatrical presentation to Roosevelt and the JCS is no fault of Wingate's. Neither Brooke nor the Chiefs of Staff argued against it, rather together with Churchill they made Wingate central to the Burma operational plan to be presented to the CCS at Quebec. They needed a positive narrative to deflect the expected criticism of the continued failure of British arms in Burma and to provide some prospect of a reopening of

---

[160] TNA, AIR 23/1944, Scoones, Lessons from Longcloth, IV Corps.
[161] TNA, AIR 23/1944, Scoones, Lessons from Longcloth, Success or Failure?

the Burma Road and to mollify Roosevelt's insistence on offering support to Chiang Kai Shek.

The Scoones Report is also quite prescient in identifying the air requirements of subsequent LRPG's. This was to be the key development coming out of Quebec with American military commitments in support of the British in India and Burma. Under the chapter on 'Air Co-operation', Scoones details the lack of proper training and preparation between 77th Brigade and the RAF, 'due to Longcloth leaders not knowing how the RAF could best provide support, and to a complete absence of training in co-operation with the air arm.'[162] This was to be admirably resolved at Quebec with the allocation of 1st Air Commando, a direct decision of both Marshall and Arnold, the Air Commando allocated to and wholly serving Wingate. A related recommendation of Scoones was that of allocating light aircraft for the evacuation of casualties, a regrettable deficiency of Longcloth recognised by Wingate, and for flying in and out specialist liaison officers, prisoners and intelligence materials as required.[163]

The allocation of light planes for such purposes was Wingate's ambition for additional air support at Quebec but General Arnold saw a much more strategic and direct military role for air support with the inception of the 1st Air Commando of the USAAF. As an aside, the fact that both Wingate and Scoones, had already identified the need for light aircraft support, surely negates the claims of air support being the initial idea of Mountbatten in his official report on SEAC.[164]

---

[162] TNA, AIR 23/1944, Scoones, Longcloth Lessons, Air Co-operation.

[163] TNA, AIR 23/1944, Scoones, Longcloth Lessons, IV Corps.

[164] Mountbatten, *Report to the Combined Chiefs of Staff,* p. 4.

Mountbatten later repeated this to Kirby, in preparation of Volume III of the *Official History*:

I asked Arnold for a complete air unit to support L.R.P. operations without disturbing the existing air forces in Burma. In particular I asked for "snatch off" gliders, light aircraft and helicopters for taking out wounded. He set up this command at once under Colonel Phil Cochrane.[165]

This account of Mountbatten's is completely at odds with the detailed American accounts of the birth of the 1st Air Commando, the personal accounts of Cochrane and Alison, the joint commanders of 1st Air Commando, and the fact that Mountbatten subsequently and privately asked Cochrane to share 1st Air Commando resources with SEAC. Cochrane produced a letter from Arnold he was given exactly for such a contingency that expressly forbid any other use of 1st Air Commando other than in direct support of Wingate.[166] This account of Cochrane's also corroborates Pogue's account of Marshall forbidding the fragmentation of 1st Air Commando resources. The American JCS in providing 1st Air Commando at the Quadrant Conference, had heavily backed Wingate to deliver in north Burma.

---

[165] TNA, CAB 101/181, Correspondence from Mountbatten to Kirby, Commentary on Chapter III, p.9, Admiral Mountbatten's Comments on Volume III of 'The Campaign in South East Asia'.

[166] USAFHRC, Colonel Philip G. Cochran, Transcript, US Air Force Oral History Interview, 20-21 October and 11th November 1975, United States Airforce Historical Research Center, pp. 191-198. <http://www.afsoc.af.mil/Portals/86/documents/history/AFD-070330-008.pdf> [accessed 14 June 2017]

If the military results of Longcloth were undeniably slight, the Operation did unquestionably raise the profile of the Burma theatre to the global agenda at Quebec, more importantly it gave the British a plausible narrative in that theatre to fend off the not wholly undeserved criticism of delay and inactivity being levelled by the Americans. The real success of Longcloth was to provide a jointly agreed strategy for Burma that served both the American and British interests, and these still did not exactly coincide. American interests were in the upper Burma Road and securing the air route to China, which at this time assumed the eventual re-conquest of all Burma, whilst British interests were in avoiding the re-conquest of Burma, if at all possible, in favour of more strategic objectives (in the British Imperial view) to the east. The compromise decisions reached at Quadrant served both interests, and further aided wider agreements regarding the Germany first strategy and friction over the timing and build -up of resources for the cross – Channel assault and disagreements over Britain's continued Mediterranean policy.

To recap on the impact of Longcloth and the myths about Wingate and the Quadrant agreement, the LRPG tactics largely created by Wingate, were already a key part of British strategy *prior* to Quadrant and clearly referenced at the Trident meetings in May. The allegation that LRPG's were wrongly seen as the solution to the re-conquest of Burma is nonsense. The LRPGs were clearly a part of the wider invasion strategy planned to secure northern Burma only. That Slim did eventually retake Burma completely was a consequence of the opportunism of a collapsing IJA after the disastrous attacks on Assam and for want of any agreed CCS position on amphibious and naval resources for South East Asia in 1944. On the eve of the momentous battles for Kohima and Imphal and Wingate's invasion of the north in Operation Thursday, Mountbatten had launched his Axiom mission to avoid an invasion of Burma, and despatched his American Chief of Staff, General Wedemeyer, to London and Washington for the purpose. This British aversion to invading Burma in favour of a Pacific focused strategy had been building further momentum since the Sextant meetings at Cairo and Tehran in late November –early December 1943, when Chiang's erratic behaviour and Stalin's insistence on both a second front and agreement to attacking Japan upon conclusion of the war in Europe, relegated the strategic importance of China in American eyes. The British staff planners assumed this relegated the Burma theatre too until Churchill, with a heavy reminder from Roosevelt, reminded his Chiefs of Staff of the commitments they had given the Americans regarding northern Burma at the Trident and Quadrant meetings the previous summer.[167]

In the lead up to Quadrant in August and concurrent with the news of Longcloth and its exploitation by British propagandists, the American impatience with British efforts and a lack of commitment had been growing. As Charles Brower asserts:

Two strategic issues, each influenced by political considerations, dominated the development of American strategy in the war with Japan during the summer of 1943: the development of a long range- plan for the defeat of Japan and the need to stimulate action in Burma to lift the siege of China.[168]

Such plans, 'directly affected, and were affected by, the

---

[167] CHAR, 20/157/117, Personal Telegram, Prime Minister to President, No. 592, 25 February 1944.
<http://www.churchillarchive.com> [accessed 1 February 2016]
[168] Charles F. Brower, *Defeating Japan: The Joint Chiefs of Staff and Strategy in the Pacific War, 1943-1945* (New York: Palgrave Macmillan, 2012), p. 39.

British; for whatever was done in China depended on India and Burma, where the C.B.I. organisation lay across British territory and the only British strategic theatre in the Far East.'[169]

At the Trident meetings in May the CCS had agreed that the Combined Staff Planners (CSP) should prepare an outline plan for the defeat of Japan. To this end the JCS sent the American contingent to London in June. The guidance for this mission was to emphasize to the British the global and interlinked aspect of the war with Japan, the need to keep China in the war and the primacy of US strategic and military leadership in the Pacific. The reports back to Washington were not encouraging. 'The absence of a British sense of urgency was infuriating.'[170]

As a result the US Joint Staff Planners (JSP) reaffirmed the vital importance of maintaining China in the war and that the recapture of Burma took precedence over any planned operations by the British in Sumatra- Malaya, and that the latter operations if and when they did take place must not interfere with US operations in the central Pacific.[171] In the weeks leading up to Quadrant the Combined Planning Staff (CPS) therefore produced an outline strategic plan for the defeat of Japan, CPS 83.[172] This was circulated together with a memorandum highlighting strategic differences for discussion

---

[169] John Ehrman, *Grand Strategy: August 1943 – September 1944, HMSO Official History of the Second World War,* 6 vols (London: HMSO, 1956), V, p. 128.

[170] Brower, p. 41.

[171] Brower, p. 42.

[172] CARL, CPS 83 'Appreciation and Plan for the Defeat of Japan', *Quadrant Conference, August 1943, Papers & Minutes of Meetings 1943* (Washington, DC: Office of the Combined Chiefs of Staff, 1943), pp. 162-170.
<http://cgsc.contentdm.oclc.org/cdm/ref/collection/p4013coll8/id/3694> [accessed 29 March 2016]

at Quadrant on 18 August 1943. The tensions over strategy between the Allies is palpable in the wording submitted for the attention of the CCS for discussion and agreement, the relevant sections were as follows:

4. On the basis of the premises adopted, the Combined Staff Planners consider that the measures set forth as being necessary for the defeat of Japan, namely, the retention of China as an effective ally, the destruction of Japanese sea and air forces, the blockade of Japan, and the large scale bombing of the Japanese homeland as a preliminary to the possible invasion of Japan, are sound.

5. The general lines of advance – through the CENTRAL and SOUTHWEST PACIFIC, and possibly in the NORTHWEST PACIFIC by UNITED STATES' forces; and through the STRAITS OF MALACCA and CHINA SEA by British forces, with the development of a line of supplies to CHINA through BURMA, are concurred in.[173]

From an American perspective three of the four measures considered necessary in point 4; the retention of China as an effective ally, the destruction of Japanese sea and air forces, and the large scale bombing of the Japanese homeland, all three required vigorous action by the British in Burma. How and when this might actually be carried out put the Allied position at loggerheads:

12. The U.S. Planners feel that our plans and preparations should contemplate the defeat of JAPAN not later than 12

---

[173] CARL, Memorandum from the Combined Planning Staff to the CCS on CPS 83 'Appreciation and Plan for the Defeat of Japan', *Quadrant Conference, August 1943, Papers & Minutes of Meetings 1943,* p. 155.
<http://cgsc.contentdm.oclc.org/cdm/ref/collection/p4013coll8/id/3694> [accessed 29 March 2016]

months after the defeat of GERMANY. This timing should itself now be established as a more or less controlling objective with which our efforts, measures and courses of action should conform [...] The British Planners, however, while fully conscious of the need to shorten the war against Japan and take all possible measures so to shorten it, cannot accept such a target date.[174]

The American planners, under the direction of Marshall and the JCS, were under pressure to devise a plan that both shortened the war against Japan and committed the British to action in Burma where few American forces, other than Stilwell's Chinese at Ledo and USAAF resources, were available. Marshall acutely felt the pressure of time and public opinion at home in insisting on a rapid conclusion of the war against Japan if it was to be pushed through to an unconditional surrender.

CPS 83 from the American perspective clearly saw the British as not doing enough and not doing it quickly enough:

15. The U.S. Planners assume that the operations in NORTH BURMA, as approved at the TRIDENT Conference – advance from LEDO and IMPHAL, and increase of supplies by air to CHINA, the AKYAB and RAMREE operations – will be firmly carried out in 1943-44. Beyond these operations the plan submitted by the British Members does not contemplate offensive operations from the WEST (other than further operations in NORTH BURMA) until March, 1945[...] The U.S. Planners feel that a more extensive contribution to the war

---

[174] CARL, Memorandum from the Combined Planning Staff to the CCS on CPS 83, p. 156.
<http://cgsc.contentdm.oclc.org/cdm/ref/collection/p4013coll8/id/3694> [accessed 29 March 2016]

is necessary along this line of advance during this period.

16. The U.S. Planners consider that Course B, the capture of SOUTH BURMA, beginning in November, 1944, should be carried out. This operation is regarded as necessary not only for the improved line of supplies to CHINA through RANGOON, but as a preliminary to the further movement of the advance from the WEST through the STRAIT OF MALACCA.[175]

The British were resolved not to be committed to the recapture of Burma other than the limited operations in the North:

18. The British Planners feel strongly that the recapture of SOUTHERN BURMA and RANGOON would be a small strategic gain for the expenditure of great effort...

19. On the other hand, the British planners feel that the recapture of SINGAPORE before RANGOON is a full and correct application of sea and air power.[176]

We can see clearly laid out in CPS 83 the struggle between the Allies over the strategy to defeat Japan. The British needed to demonstrate commitment in Burma in support of the American strategy but they needed to do it in way that didn't overcommit resources in a theatre so starved of the materials for making war. The planning struggles over CPS 83 had their inception at Trident with the directive given at the 90th meeting of the CCS on 20 May 1943. The combined planning staff working in London in June and in Washington in July, completed CPS 83 on 8 August.[177] The British, fully aware of

---

[175] CARL, Memorandum on CPS 83, p. 157.
<http://cgsc.contentdm.oclc.org/cdm/ref/collection/p4013coll8/id/3694> [accessed 29 March 2016]

[176] CARL, Memorandum on CPS 83, p. 158.
<http://cgsc.contentdm.oclc.org/cdm/ref/collection/p4013coll8/id/3694> [accessed 29 March 2016]

[177] CARL, Memorandum on CPS 83, p. 154.

the differences and difficulties they would have with the Americans, needed to make a good impression at Quadrant and Wingate was deliberately selected to be a part of this as he was unquestionably committed to fighting the Japanese in Burma and had hugely favourable Allied publicity behind him.

The Joint Staff Mission in Washington had alerted the British delegation as to what to expect from the American negotiators:

There is an increasing feeling with U.S. Chiefs that we do not mean business in Burma, and have never meant business in Burma. We think you will find rigid insistence on everything possibly being done in that theatre, and that there will be an effort to back up demand for maximum action in Burma by absurd calculations as to possibilities of opening up road communications with Burma. Undoubtedly they will be bitterly disappointed at very modest results that, according to latest papers from London, would appear likely this winter.[178]

This was corroborated in General Alan Brooke's diary entry of 11 August, the same day that he also examined Wingate's proposals for the Burma campaign. Having been put in the picture by the JSM as to the likely American position on strategy and planned operations, he noted, 'I am not looking forward to this coming meeting, and feel we shall have a very difficult time.'[179]

Churchill was clear what he wanted out of the Quebec discussions regarding Burma; LRP operations in upper Burma, an assault on Sumatra, and the abandonment of Bullfrog, the

---

<http://cgsc.contentdm.oclc.org/cdm/ref/collection/p4013coll8/id/3694> [accessed 29 March 2016]

[178] Michael Howard, *Grand Strategy: August 1942 – September 1943, HMSO Official History of the Second World War,* 6 vols (London: HMSO, 1970), p. 563.

[179] AlanBrooke, *War Diaries*, p. 439.

planned operations against Japanese position in the south on Akyab and Ramree Island. His objectives didn't address the practical objectives of logistical feasibility, commitments to allies or a long term strategy for the defeat of Japan.[180]

General Auchinleck, the new Commander in Chief, with Wavell having been made Viceroy, was urging a larger build - up of forces in Assam and further delays to British action in Burma. Churchill was enraged and in two forceful papers to the Chiefs of Staff on 24 and 26 July, 'he castigated both the command in India and the pointlessness of the operations for which such ponderous resources were now being required.'[181] Against this backdrop of American mistrust and British inactivity, Wingate had emerged from the jungle a hero and Churchill milked the opportunity to try and do something positive in the Burma theatre, but more importantly, to be seen by the Americans to be doing so.

According to Howard, in Churchill's calculations:

A strong feature could be made of overland assault from Assam and Yunnan to open the Burma Road. It might reconcile the Americans to the abandonment of Akyab – an unsound operation anyway, using up shipping for what he now called the "Torch" of Asia – "Culverin"; the sweeping amphibious movement directed south – eastward towards Singapore.[182]

This brings us back to the question as to what did Operation Longcloth actually achieve? Militarily it is quite indisputable that very little was achieved other than refining and further innovating the concept of supplying by air an armed force in the field. It is self-evident that from a morale boosting perspective it was enormously successful and even Slim grudgingly

---

[180] Howard, pp. 571 - 72.

[181] Howard, p. 546.

[182] Howard, p. 549.

recognised this aspect of the operation, annotating on Barton's draft narrative of Longcloth for the Official History:

Its chief functional value was the use F.M. Slim and other commanders in Burma made of it to point out if one lot could beat Japs in Jungle so could rest.[183]

However, from a strategic perspective Longcloth had an enormous and quite under - appreciated impact on both the British and the Americans. The impact on the Japanese has already been dealt with earlier in this chapter and despite Slim's claims to the contrary, the *Japanese Monograph* testimony is a convincing narrative as to how Longcloth impacted on the enemy's strategic concept for the defence of Burma. Regarding British and American proposed and planned strategy, the historical facts and series of events leading up to and unfolding at the Quebec Conference, demonstrate that the British Army establishment view and that of the *Official History* is a disservice to the memory and achievements of Wingate. The accepted or 'Establishment' narrative is that Wingate's forceful and difficult character beguiled the British Prime Minister, his Chiefs of Staff, the CIGS, the American President, his Joint Chiefs of Staff, and the Staff Planners who haggled with Auchinleck through June to August 1943.

The British had to demonstrate a commitment to Burma operations at Quadrant even if those operations were biased towards an American concept of strategy for the defeat of Japan. The British delegation were reminded of this in no uncertain terms on 20 August with a memo from the United States Chiefs of Staff, CCS 313/1, amending the minutes of CCS 313, on the Appreciation and Plan for the Defeat of Japan. The JCS wanted reaffirmation in paragraph 20 of the Trident decisions that

---

[183] TNA, CAB 106/206, Slim to Barton, Narrative on Operations of Special Force.

approved operations in north Burma and against Akyab and Ramree for the coming dry season, measures to aid the war effort of China and as a base of operations, maximum expansion of air supply to China, and planning for the conquest of Southern Burma and / or Malaya in 1944.[184]

In reality, the perception of British proactive operations in upper Burma and its future potential to do so gave Churchill and the British strategic options with the Americans, not just in the Far East but globally. By demonstrating a commitment in upper Burma to support American strategy Churchill hoped to avoid a costly campaign to retake the whole of Burma and in doing so to save British resources. These would then be used to push eastwards to have a say in the Pacific campaign that was almost totally the preserve of the Americans and to retake British Imperial possessions in Malaysia and Singapore. British planning for a Pacific involvement accelerated significantly after Sextant when it appeared to the British they might be free of any pressing commitment in Burma until Roosevelt insisted in February 1944.[185]

A further global strategic perspective was the balance of resources between theatres, and after manpower the most frequently debated resource was landing craft. Any British move across the Bay of Bengal either to Rangoon or bypassing

---

[184] CARL, CCS 313/1 *Quadrant Conference, August 1943, Papers & Minutes of Meetings 1943*, pp. 171-172.
<http://cgsc.contentdm.oclc.org/cdm/ref/collection/p4013coll8/id/3694> [accessed 29 March 2016]

[185] NARA, FDR Library, Map Room Papers, Box 5, Roosevelt to Churchill February 1944, From the President to the Former Naval Person, No. 480, 24 February 1944. Franklin D. Roosevelt Library and Museum Website, version dated 2016. <http://www.fdrlibrary.marist.edu/_resources/images/mr/mr0030.pdf> [accessed 10 April 2017]

Burma required this precious resource. There were insufficient landing craft to fulfil the needs of the British preferred Mediterranean strategy and the American preferred cross channel strategy together with the extensive ongoing and planned American Pacific operations. Amphibious operations by the British in Burma or in the Bay of Bengal would always be a low priority for the Allies and Chiang probably knew this when making such an operation conditional on his support of Chinese forces in Burma.

Thus, British commitment to the war with Japan could only be demonstrated to the Americans by action in upper Burma, which coincided with the American concept and control of the air war against Japan. The Air Plan for the Defeat of Japan, CCS 323, was circulated at the CCS 114th Meeting on 21 August, the last agenda item of the day, and was referred after discussion to the Combined Staff Planners for further study and to report back to the CCS by 15 September.[186] Contained in this remarkable document is the meat of what Brower described as getting the British to bend to the American concept of strategy in a theatre not in their control. The mission of CCS 323 was:

To accomplish, by a combined aerial offensive, the destruction of the Japanese military, industrial and economic systems to such a degree that the nation's capacity for armed resistance is effectively eliminated within 12 months of the defeat of Germany.[187]

---

[186] CARL, CCS 114, 21 August 1943, *Quadrant Conference, August 1943, Papers & Minutes of Meetings 1943*, p. 477. <http://cgsc.contentdm.oclc.org/cdm/ref/collection/p4013coll8/id/3694> [accessed 29 March 2016]

[187] CARL, CCS 323, 20 August 1943, *Quadrant Conference, August 1943, Papers & Minutes of Meetings 1943*, p. 289. <http://cgsc.contentdm.oclc.org/cdm/ref/collection/p4013coll8/id/3694> [accessed 29 March 2016]

Of the six operating assumptions for success set out in this paper, four required a much more proactive attitude from the British forces in Assam and Burma; keeping China as an active ally, expanding the air, road and pipeline facilities, applying constant pressure on Japanese forces in October 1944 – August 1945, and finally, north and north central Burma cleared of the enemy and occupied in 1944 and all of Burma in 1945. This wasn't Churchill's vision of a British Far East strategy.

The Air Plan was grand in design; at its full operating capacity having 4000 B24s supplying 784 B29's based in China, and in range of the Japanese Home Islands. These B24's would operate from 54 Indian aerodromes (of which 10 currently existed) to 50 staging aerodromes in Kunming and then on to Changsha to maintain and supply the B29 force at 20 new aerodromes. The map summarising these operations is attached to CCS 323. The flight corridor of the B24 base area in Calcutta and the staging area in Kunming is one that contains Myitkyina; this was Stilwell's objective, and was to become Special Force's stated support role in Operation Thursday.[188]

The ambition of the US strategic bombing campaign planned as a key part of the wider strategy for the defeat of Japan is a far more compelling argument for General Arnold's generous supply of a combined air wing for Wingate's sole use rather than the persuasive powers of Mountbatten.

In reassessing the impact of Longcloth, although the immediate military contribution was negligible, the impact on Allied strategy in both Burma and Europe was significant. The

---

[188] CARL, CCS 323, 20 August 1943, *Quadrant Conference, August 1943, Papers & Minutes of Meetings 1943*, p. 300-301. <http://cgsc.contentdm.oclc.org/cdm/ref/collection/p4013coll8/id/3694> [accessed 29 March 2016]

leverage of Longcloth at the Quadrant Conference was not simply a grand gesture of Churchill's and the grateful opportunism of Wingate, it was a deliberate positioning of an already planned support role of Wingate's forces. A role that was planned by Wavell, by IV Corps within Fourteenth Army, and enhanced by General Alan Brooke and the British COS in the days leading up to Quadrant. The oft maligned personality of Wingate was a refreshingly positive one in contrast to Wavell's performance at Trident regarding the Burma theatre but it is incidental to the events that saw the commitment of the Chindits to an enlarged and more important strategic role.

Chapter Four: Field Marshal Slim and the negative judgement of the Chindits.

'Of course we differed on many things. It was impossible not to differ from a man who so fanatically pursued his own purposes without regard to any other consideration or person.'[189]

When assessing the Chindits, Slim's *Defeat into Victory* and his contributions to the *Official Histories,* were both in direct contradiction to the eulogies he had uttered a decade or more earlier in 1944 and to his expressed opinions at the time. This contradictory approach was confusing to both Chindit veterans and the general public alike. In 1944 Slim had written on hearing of Wingate's death that, 'The number of men of our race who are really irreplaceable can be counted on the fingers of one hand. Wingate is one of them.'[190] But by 1956 Slim's assessments had become pointedly critical both personally and professionally, 'I think that Wingate regarded *himself* as a prophet, and that always leads to a single-centredness that verges on fanaticism, with all its faults.'[191] In his concluding remarks on the Chindits in *Defeat into Victory,* Slim recorded:

I came firmly to the conclusion that such formations, trained, equipped, and mentally adjusted for one kind of operation only, were wasteful. They did not give, militarily, a worthwhile return

---

[189] Slim, p. 248.
[190] Slim, The Chindits SEAC Pamphlet, 1944, quoted in Trevor Royle, *Orde Wingate: A Man of Genius 1903-1944* (London: Weidenfeld & Nicolson, 1995; repr. 2010), p. 314.
[191] Slim, p. 308.

for the resources in men, material and time they absorbed.[192]

Writing in 1959, Christopher Sykes offered an assessment of Slim's views of Wingate which were no doubt shared by many former Chindits:

Defeat into Victory [...] is a memorable work written with the skill of a born writer, but the student of Wingate must read it with perplexity. Throughout the record the Field Marshal adopts a detached and modest tone, and his general picture of the defeat of 1942 and the subsequent Burma campaigns culminating in the re-conquest seems to be impeccable, yet when the same man comes to write of Wingate he is at such extraordinary variance with the memories and opinions of others, and in contradiction with so much ascertainable fact, that it is hard to resist the impression that on this subject the Field-Marshal's mind is not wholly free of prejudice.[193]

Yet, even before Slim was to set out his opinions and assessment of Wingate and the Chindits there was a clear precedent in these views of the Fourteenth Army leadership, written as early as 1945 by General Giffard, Commander -in - Chief, 11 Army Group, South East Asia Command. Giffard wrote in a report to the Secretary for War, in relation to Operation Thursday:

I have nothing but praise for the organisation of the initial landings, and the gallantry and endurance displayed by all ranks in the operations which followed. Events have shown, however, that these operations had less effect upon the enemy than I had hoped for. The enemy did not divert troops from his forward areas, nor did he alter his main strategical plan. In fact, the results achieved did not prove to be commensurate with the

---

[192] Slim, p. 625.

[193] Christopher H. Sykes, *Orde Wingate* (London: Collins, 1959), p. 17.

expenditure in manpower and material which had been employed.[194]

Defeat into Victory was published in 1956 and was written with the full benefit of hindsight. It must be remembered that the outcome of the war was uncertain in 1943-44 and Slim's reputation was yet to be established. The comments made by Slim on Special Force's achievements are almost verbatim to those made by Giffard in his official report eleven years earlier. Slim's views are therefore consistent despite what the public perception created might be regarding Wingate, and Slim was in a position of influence to correct what he thought to be an historical distortion of his own central contribution to the Burma victory. The subsequent evidence presented here certainly suggests that Slim was forceful and unwavering in this respect and that Kirby was simply more a willing agent rather than the principal in this process. Slim appears to the main driver.

Brian Bond makes a very acute observation on the immediate post war image of Slim:

Wingate was the equivalent of T.E. Lawrence in the First World War, his deeds and controversial personality overshadowing Slim's achievement as Lawrence's has done to Allenby's. Even after the Second World War, Slim's had not become a household name in Britain despite his ascent to the head of the Army (CIGS) in 1948. He had made only a fleeting appearance in the popular film *Burma Victory* and was, in

---

[194] General Sir George J. Giffard, 'Despatch on Operations in Burma and North – East India, 16 November 1943 to 22 June 1944: submitted to Secretary of State for War on 19th June 1945', in *Despatches from the Front: The Battle for Burma 1943-45, from Kohima & Imphal Through to Victory*, ed. by John Grehan & Martin Mace (Barnsley: Pen & Sword, 2015), pp. 1-62 (p.28).

effect, squeezed out of public attention by the more controversial characters and exploits of Mountbatten and Wingate. [195]

As Duncan Anderson describes in *Churchill's Generals,* 'It is all too easy to forget that when Wingate was killed in March 1944 Slim had only one victory to his credit, a minor action against the Vichy French in Syria in July 1940, and that the list of his defeats was very long.'[196]

This lack of both public and official recognition of Slim was present at the highest levels of government. Slim was never Churchill's favourite general despite the fact that he had famously destroyed a Japanese army in Burma and inflicted upon the Imperial Japanese Army its greatest ever land defeat. Despite the scale of British victory, it was a land battle that Churchill never wanted, for he had always favoured an amphibious flank attack via Rangoon, or even bypassing Burma completely. The icy relations lingered on after of the war. In July 1952 Slim, who had been CIGS since 1948, lobbied Churchill to reassess the role and status of Fourteenth Army in Volume V of the latter's *History of the Second World War.* Churchill, in private correspondence to Sir Henry Pownall, wrote:

Slim told me the other day that he had a good many letters from the Fourteenth Army about there being no mention of the Fourteenth Army in Volume V. The Corps are mentioned but not the Army. They complain it is not even in the index and is

---

[195] Brian Bond, 'The Army Level of Command: General Sir William Slim and Fourteenth Army in Burma', in *British and Japanese Military Leadership in the Far Eastern War 1941-4*, ed. by Brian Bond and Kyoichi Tachikawa (Abingdon: Routledge, 2012), pp. 38-52 (p. 39).

[196] Duncan Anderson, 'Slim', in *Churchill's Generals*, ed. by John Keegan (London: Cassell, 2005), pp. 298-322 (p. 300).

given no collective status such as was so freely given to the Eighth Army.[197]

Lord Mountbatten, in terms of immediate post- war reputation, also overshadowed that of Slim's. As the Supreme Allied Commander in South East Asia, his was the responsibility to implement the strategy of the British Chiefs of Staff and the Allied Combined Chiefs of Staff. The British long -term interest in Burma was getting to Singapore and restoring possession of the pre -war colonies in the Far East. As we have established already the American interest in Burma related directly and solely to its 'China first' strategy and was actively opposed to British efforts to re-establish the pre -war colonial status quo.

With Operation Buccaneer (the amphibious assault across the Bay of Bengal), cancelled after the Cairo Conference in December 1943, and despite some amphibious assaults towards Malaya late in the war when Japan was all but beaten, Mountbatten's real success in theatre was mostly Slim's in strategy and execution. This would not be evident to Churchill in reading Mountbatten's reports. With the crossing of the Chindwin and widespread advance of British formations under Slim's Fourteenth Army, an appreciation of the strategy and dispositions by Mountbatten in January 1945 makes not one reference to Slim in its three pages.[198] Mountbatten's Report to

---

[197] CHAR, 4/341, WSC to Sir Henry Pownall, Corrections: comments and queries on First Edition and proofs of Volume 5, on comment from Field Marshal Sir William Slim that the Fourteenth Army was not mentioned by name in Volume 5, Image 8 of 185.
<http://www.churchillarchive.com> [accessed 1 February 2016]
[198] CHAR, 20/211/36-38, Telegram from Lord Louis Mountbatten to WSC marked "Personal" reporting on his visit

the CCS, first published in 1947, shows that whilst it was generous to the contributions of various parties involved in SEAC, it has his own supposed military genius and dynamic leadership at its centre.[199] Slim's lack of wider public profile in the immediate post war period was not helped by his C in C at SEAC.

Slim had himself been temporarily sacked in 1945 by General Oliver Leese, prior to the final advance on Rangoon, a decision in which Mountbatten was complicit in his acquiescence. The near threat of mutiny in Fourteenth Army and the good sense of Sir Alan Brooke reversed this decision quickly. Anderson comments on this period, '..it was easier for the government to attribute that success to the new men they had appointed – Leese and Mountbatten.'[200]

By the time of the remorseless advance towards Rangoon in late 1944 and 1945 the Americans had lost much of their strategic interest in northern Burma. The island hopping campaign in the Pacific had already secured both a more direct route to the invasion of the Japanese mainland and a platform for launching General Arnold's Strategic Air Forces, in his VLR Bomber Programme, spearheaded by the newly introduced B-29 bomber. The debacle of General Chennault's air strategy had been revealed in mid-1944 as the Chindits were toiling against the Japanese in Mogaung, under Stilwell's

---

to the Fourteenth Army Front in Burma: stating that he is confident of a major defeat of the Japanese in this area, in addition to the capture of Mandalay [Burma]; and emphasising the high morale and superiority of Allied forces, 23 January 1945.
<http://www.churchillarchive.com> [accessed 1 February 2016]
[199] Mountbatten, *Report to the Combined Chiefs of Staff*, p. 50.
[200] Anderson, p. 300.

distant and uncomprehending direction of Brigadier Michael Calvert's diminished and dwindling 77th Brigade. Chennault, always at odds with Stilwell, had insisted on strategic airbases and B29s operating out of India and China, but without any meaningful ground forces required to secure those bases in China. The Japanese swiftly overran these bases in Operation Ichi-Go and severely curtailed Arnold's 'Matterhorn' VLR bomber plan.

Thus, by 1945 Burma had become an even lower priority in American eyes. The Pacific was a more fruitful campaign in defeating Japan, Chiang's star was waning with Roosevelt, finally, if somewhat belatedly, and China was no longer essential to the VLR bomber campaign for the smashing of Japan's industries. As a global bargaining chip Burma no longer had much currency. Operation Overlord in Europe had much delayed Britain's Burma invasion plans due to shipping and landing craft shortages, but immediate American objectives had been met in the seizure of Myitkyina in August 1944. This was seen as the pivotal achievement to secure both the air route against Japanese attack and linking the Ledo Road to the old Burma Road. Thereafter Burma and the wider campaign was of less interest in Washington as a means to bringing about the defeat of Japan.

As described by Slim in *Defeat into Victory*, the 1945 campaign was one achieved by British Commonwealth forces, albeit with very significant American air resources, without which the advance would not have been possible. If there was little interest in the 'forgotten army' back in Britain there was arguably even less interest in Washington by 1945. In 1943 and early 1944 though, the proactively bellicose attitude and exploits of Wingate and the Chindits had resonated with American objectives. They were lauded, and continue to be so in American military appreciations of their combined forces role with the 1st Air Commando, which was both General Arnold's and General Marshall's personal commitment to get the British moving aggressively in Burma. In this context Slim's reputation was far below that of Wingate and Mountbatten in senior military eyes in Washington, at least. It took a decade of reflection and enhanced reputation building to change this in British eyes and both *Defeat into Victory* and the *Official Histories* were to play a vital part, yet the American narratives on Burma, especially the numerous war college theses, still tend to lionise the part played by Wingate, in conjunction with 1st Air Commando.

Writing in *National Geographic* in August 1944 on the campaign in Burma, General Arnold said:

In 1943 British Major General Orde C. Wingate led a daring campaign against the Japanese in Burma. He proved that Allied ground troops could operate behind the enemy's lines, cutting off his supply system and upsetting his schedule. General Wingate marched fast and struck hard. The enemy, never knowing where he was going to strike next, completely thrown off balance. Indeed, this British general's behind-the-lines operations in Burma brought to mind the brilliant cavalry manoeuvers of Nathan Bedford Forrest in our own Civil War. In 1944 General Wingate wished to lead another expedition into Burma on a larger scale. Previously he had to leave some of his sick and wounded behind his swiftly moving columns, but in 1944 he wanted to fly all of them to safety. We promised we would do that - and more.[201]

Arnold went on to describe the cooperation of the Allies as follows:

Co-operating with the Army Air Force in this project were a

---

[201] General Henry H. Arnold, 'The Aerial Invasion of Burma', *National Geographic*, 86 (August 1944), 129-148.

British Army unit under Lt. Gen W. J. Slim, the Indian forces under General Wingate, the tactical air forces under Air Marshal Sir John Baldwin and the Troop Carrier Command under Brig Gen William D. Old, of the U.S. Army. All would work together.

One can only speculate at what Slim and the Indian Army establishment made of this assessment by the head of the USAAF and member of the CCS that it was Wingate's show and Slim is responsible for only a "British Army unit".

The concluding comments in Arnold's article restate the centrality of Wingate to the current campaign:

At this writing, it is too early to estimate the military significance of this operation, except to say that its successful execution gave a terrific lift to all Allied operations in the China-Burma-India theatre. Many lessons were learned that will be valuable in the future. The able General Wingate was killed in March of this year in an airplane crash, *but his good work continues.* (This writer's emphasis).

Clearly we can see from General Arnold's article, published five months after Wingate's death, that in his view, Wingate was the main player in Allied operations and Slim was viewed as only a supporting actor.

In private correspondence in 1952 with Lieutenant Colonel H. R. K. Gibbs, who was writing a history of the 6th Gurkha Rifles,[202] and was seeking Slim's advice on the draft narrative, Slim offered the following clear and unequivocal opinion on the chain of command as it related to Burma operations; 'You have somewhere else the remark that part of the Chindits returned to the Fourteenth Army. They and Stilwell's Chinese and Americans were part of Fourteenth Army under my command

---

[202] Lieutenant Colonel H. R. K. Gibbs, *Historical Record of the 6th Gurkha Rifles* (Aldershot: Gale & Polden, 1955).

for practically all the time of your narrative.'[203] It is quite likely that this issue of the fact and fiction of reputation, leadership and responsibility was a recurring and irksome one to Slim – and it started at the top with no less a man than General Arnold! The fact that Gibbs, a fellow Gurkha, also made the same assumptions as Arnold shows that this under appreciation of Slim relative to Wingate was not just one of public opinion. Peter Mead points out in his work, *Orde Wingate and the Historians,* that Gibbs's account was the last one to be free of criticism of Wingate before *Defeat into Victory,* despite Slim's negative comments on the draft narrative to Gibbs.

There is a fascinating contemporary document from November 1944 discovered in the private papers of a Medical Orderly with 81st West African Division that fought in the Arakan and had also provided a contingent for Wingate's Special Force upon arrival in India in November 1943. This Pamphlet, titled *'Jungle Commando: The Story of the West African Expeditionary Forces First Campaign in Burma'*, was prepared and published by the Public Relations Branch, General Headquarters, West Africa and issued by East Africa Command.[204] The 81st West African Division are notably not a part of the Indian Army establishment and were the only

---

[203] Imperial War Museum, London [Hereafter IWM], Misc. 54, Item 824, Field Marshal Viscount Slim to Lt. Col. H. R. K. Gibbs, 1942-1963, Commentary notes for page 131, from Slim on Gibbs draft narrative of 6th Gurkha Rifles, 3 pages, 14 July 1952, p. 3.

[204] J.D. Atwell Private Papers, East Africa Command Pamphlet, Nov. 1944, 'Jungle Commando: The Story of the West African Expeditionary Forces First Campaign in Burma', in Unpublished Private Papers of J. D. Atwell, M. O., 6 Field Ambulance, West Africa Army Medical Corps, 81st West African Division.

external dominion force to serve with Fourteenth Army. This official publication has some interesting comments regarding Wingate which are fundamentally different to those of Slim and the Fourteenth Army hierarchy.

On Wingate's character it notes that:

To understand the story of the West Africans' campaign it is essential to know certain principles of warfare which were developed for use in the jungle by a brilliant and original leader of men – the late General Wingate.[205]

On Wingate's theories as applied to the 81st Division, the pamphlet describes how the Division was maintained through the Arakan campaign, (note – not the Chindit campaign in the north):

The West Africans, for the first time in the Burma fighting, applied the Wingate theory to a much larger force, numbering many thousands of men. They fought a regular campaign, lived exclusively on supplies dropped from the air (on the Wingate model) and then returned to their base, still a complete formation, when the coming of the monsoon made further operations impossible.

But the bold idea succeeded. The West Africans never once went supperless to bed, and every sick and wounded man was taken out of the bush by air, often under the fire of the Japanese, from strips and landing grounds the troops made as they fought.[206]

Where Slim avers that Wingate's methods were merely copying current practice and thinking, the 81st West African Division sees the credit being Wingate's. This document is a

---

[205] Atwell Private Papers, East Africa Command Pamphlet, p. 4.
[206] Atwell Private Papers, East Africa Command Pamphlet, p. 5.

good example of the digression of opinion about Wingate amongst British forces in 1944. The 81st West African Division certainly underlines the high reputation of Wingate at this time in finding a way to successfully fight the Japanese.

Within this immediate wartime and early post - war context was it more than this natural desire to build his own historical reputation against such prevailing views that prompted Slim to 'correct' the misconception of Wingate as the hero of Burma's liberation? Could it have been more personal?

In Brigadier Michael Calvert's oral history, recorded for the IWM, he offers a reconciliatory and kindly appreciation of Slim's negative views of Wingate in *Defeat into Victory*. Recounting a meeting with Slim in the 1960s, Calvert said that Slim regretted what had been published about Wingate. This was related to the fact that Brigadier Michael Roberts had ghost written significant portions of the narrative and was also attached to the Cabinet Office Historical Section in compiling the *Official History*. After Roberts's death Calvert recounts that Slim told him that his book, 'took a wrong turn regarding Wingate and that he was not in agreement but he was too busy and didn't have time to stop it or amend it.'[207]

Slim was perhaps being overly diplomatic with Calvert, a diehard Wingate supporter, with a tempestuous reputation that was well earned both in and out of uniform. It is instructive to look at the time scale of these comments by Slim. The meeting with Calvert was in the late 1960s and *Defeat into Victory* was published in 1956. Writing to Gibbs in July 1952 Slim had offered that:

I doubt if Wingate was altogether a genius. He had flashes of genius but he had some pretty black spots too. However, I

---

[207] IWM, Cat No. 9942, Calvert Oral Interview, Reel 18, 1'30"-2'40".

wouldn't alter your book. The trouble is no one will write what they really think about him.[208]

Calvert did note that Roberts was Slim's Intelligence Officer in Burma, and who for whatever reason, he believed he held a grudge against Wingate to the extent that he displayed, 'an unmilitary attitude' towards the Chindit leader.[209] Despite Slim's comment to Gibbs in 1952, write about Wingate what they really thought, Roberts and Slim certainly did in the next few years. The comments to Gibbs were four years before *Defeat into Victory* and nine years before Volume III of the *Official History*. It is difficult not to conclude that the denigration of Wingate was deliberate on the part of both Slim and Roberts.

Elsewhere in the correspondence with Gibbs, there are other proposed alterations to his draft narrative that are given by Slim, that preceded the drafting of both *Defeat into Victory* and the *Official History,* which doesn't reflect favourably on Slim regarding his protests to Calvert as to the 'wrong turn' in the drafting of his book. A number of the comments were to become recurring themes in the Slim and Kirby narratives, such as the supposed innovation of air supply and ground to air tactics, 'Wingate saw the use of air transport but so did most other people.'[210] Slim also raises the issue of Wingate's ego and desire for an expanded role for LRP as the main force, 'He wanted it (the L.R.P. force) as the <u>main</u> force all else subsidiary

---

[208] IWM, Misc. 54, Item 824, Field Marshal Viscount Slim to Lt. Col. H. R. K. Gibbs, Commentary notes for page 119, from Slim to Gibbs, p. 1.

[209] IWM, Cat No. 9942, Calvert Oral Interview, Reel 18, 0'10".

[210] IWM, Misc. 54, Item 824, Field Marshal Viscount Slim to Lt. Col. H. R. K. Gibbs, Commentary notes for page 120.

– a nonsense.'[211]

Another well-known story that reflected badly on Wingate was Slim's version of the hastily convened conference at Hailakandi airfield (as Slim recalled) prior to the fly-in for Operation Thursday when 1st Air Commando photo reconnaissance had spotted logs at the Piccadilly landing site. In Slim's version of this to Gibbs in 1952 he suggests Wingate 'urged very strongly that the whole fly in should be cancelled.'[212] This developed into a narrative about Wingate being hysterical and over emotional by the time it appeared in *Defeat into Victory* in 1956. Slim records that, 'Wingate was now in a very emotional state, and to avoid discussion with him before an audience, I drew him to one side.' [213] Slim's description of Wingate's behaviour on the night of the fly-in and his lack of assuredness in his decision making was not backed up by other observers, such as Air Marshal Baldwin, Major General Tulloch, Brigadier Calvert, Brigadier Scott and Sir Robert Thompson. In Slim's account of this story to Gibbs he recounts that he and Jack Baldwin commanding 3rd Tactical Air Force were the only senior commanders present at the airfield conference.[214]

Sir Robert Thompson's own version of this incident is as follows:

Mike was called over for a discussion with Wingate, Cochrane, Alison and Scottie. The rest of us stood in the background. The real decision was left to and was reached by Mike, Scottie and Alison, who were the three to go on and that

---

[211] IWM, Misc. 54, Item 824, Commentary notes for page 120.
[212] IWM, Misc. 54, Item 824, Commentary notes for page 130.
[213] Slim, pp. 298-299.
[214] IWM, Misc. 54, Item 824, Commentary notes for page 130, from Slim to Gibbs, p. 2.

we should switch to Broadway alone. Wingate and Cochrane supported this and Wingate went over to get the agreement of Slim and Baldwin.

There have been many accounts of this episode and the writers of the *Official History* wanted to use one that would have supported the denigration of Wingate but it was shot down by Air Marshal Baldwin.[215]

Also as Rooney has pointed out, Slim's recollection of events is demonstrably flawed as the initial fly –in was from Lalaghat airfield and not Hailakandi.[216] The latter airfield was one of three used for Operation Thursday, 'Flights were flown from three airfields, Hailakandi and Lalaghat in Assam and Tulihal in the Imphal plain. All glider operations would be mounted from Lalaghat.'[217] Compare this with Slim's narrative in *Defeat into Victory*, 'On the morning of 5 March, I circled the landing ground at Hailakandi. Below me, at the end of the wide brown airstrip, was parked a great flock of squat, clumsy gliders, their square wing –tips almost touching; around the edges of the field stood the more graceful Dakotas that were to lift them into the sky.'[218] That is a rather fundamental error in the recounting of a key event in the Burma campaign and the largest ever Allied glider operation of the War prior to D-Day. This error was evident in 1952 in Slim's note to Gibbs, when Slim recounted,

---

[215] Sir Robert Thompson, KBE, *Make for the Hills* (London: Pen & Sword, 1989), p. 47.

[216] David Rooney, *Burma Victory: Imphal, Kohima and the Chindit Issue, March 1944 to May 1945* (London: Arms & Armour, 1992), p. 124.

[217] Operation Thursday, Second Chindit Expedition 1944, The Plan, Chindits Old Comrades Association.

< http://www.chindits.info/Thursday/OperationThursday.htm> [accessed 21 June 2017]

[218] Slim, pp. 295-296.

'Neither Giffard nor Mountbatten were at Hailakandi. Jack Baldwin commanding 3 T.A.F. and I were the only senior commanders.'[219] This was also repeated in *Defeat into Victory* in 1956. Anyone familiar with Chindit operations would have known this basic fact, and it suggests that Roberts was less than diligent in his research for the drafting of Slim's memoirs when it came to the Chindit perspective and facts.

Kirby raised these points about the fly –in of 77th Brigade in correspondence with Slim in preparation of Volume III of the *Official History:*

You will note that my story of the scene at Lalaghat airfield at the start of the fly-in of 77th Brigade does not quite agree with yours […] What does seem certain from the information that I have and from the photographs taken at the time, that you were not in the group around the photograph of Piccadilly when first received. The initial discussion took place with Cochrane, Allison, Baldwin, Tulloch, Wingate, Calvert, Scott and one or two others; and it was only after maybe five minutes of discussion that Wingate, Baldwin and I think Cochrane walked over to see you to obtain your decision.[220]

Slim's response to Kirby dismissed the accounts of most of those present at this scene, 'All those present were excited, some very much so, and many of them, under great personal strain. Baldwin appeared to me at the time the least disturbed and is probably the best witness.'[221] Kirby, in the event, refrained from using Slim's version of events in the *Official*

---

[219] IWM, Misc. 54, Item 824, Commentary notes for page 130, from Slim to Gibbs, p. 2.

[220] TNA, CAB 101/185, Kirby to Slim, private correspondence on draft of Vol. 3 *Official History*, 31 December 1957, p. 2.

[221] TNA, CAB 101/185, Slim to Kirby, Private Correspondence on draft of Vol. 3 *Official History*, 5 February 1958, p. 2.

History account of the fly-in.[222]

It is also helpful to contrast what Baldwin had to say on the issue of air operations in contrast to Slim's later comments that Wingate's impact on air supply was of little consequence. Writing in 1945 Baldwin commented on the combined air-ground operations as follows:

I would like to take this opportunity of paying a tribute to General Wingate and to warn people not to be drawn into a discussion of what did Wingate's first operation achieve? What did his second achieve? We cannot judge them like that. He taught us in the first place how to defeat this jungle barrier, and he certainly taught the Air Force, and, I think, the Indian Army how to work together and how to get rid of some of our phobias. He bumped our heads together and got us and the ground forces working absolutely as one, and he did this in a very short time. That is the main theme on which his operations should be judged, and not on what they achieved, although he did achieve a tremendous amount in the second.[223]

Barton's notes of an interview with Slim, in preparation for the *Official History,* repeat what was said to Gibbs, 'We learnt little new in the way of air supply, which we had already tested and nothing of air transportation of troops.'[224] This consistent position of Slim's regarding Wingate's contribution (or lack thereof) to the development of air supply and transportation does not accord with Baldwin's assessment of his impact on the combined efforts of the air and ground forces in Burma.

---

[222] Kirby, *Official History*, III, p. 179.

[223] TNA, CAB 101/ 184, Air Marshall Baldwin, 'Certain Aspects of Air Warfare in Burma', Lecture 21 March 1945, Extracts from the Wingate Papers.

[224] TNA, CAB 106/206, J. E. E. Barton, Notes on Meeting with Field Marshall Slim, Comments on First Chindit Expedition, 1953.

An interesting perspective on Slim's views on Special Force are provided by General Symes, the former commanding officer of the 70th Indian Division, prior to its break up under instruction from the Chiefs of Staff after the Quadrant agreement in August 1943. General Symes's subsequent notes of his interrogation of Japanese prisoners in January 1946 may be cynically interpreted as a deliberately positive search for affirmation of the contribution of the Chindit operations.[225] In fact Slim himself did infer this in his correspondence to Gibbs in 1952. Slim wrote:

I know some people claim on the strength of a Jap prisoner interrogation that the 1st expedition stopped a Japanese offensive towards India. I don't think it did at all. The Japs weren't strong enough then to launch one anyway – they only had four divisions in all Burma.[226]

Here, Slim is either deliberately misleading Gibbs in his recounting of the interview or had not sufficiently read or understood it. The Symes interrogation actually records that:

At the time, 18 Div. were training for an operation planned for early 1944 –i.e. an advance from Myitkyina northwards into Assam, and directed on Tinsukia (Comment: They were quite insistent on this). The Wingate Expedition changed this. It showed them that if the British could cross from the east across the Chindwin, they likewise could go westwards against Imphal and Kohima. The Tinsukia plan was accordingly scrapped.[227]

As we know subsequently, the Japanese attacks did come in

---

[225] TNA, WO 106/4827, General G. W. Symes, Japanese Prisoner Interrogation, 'Some Views on the Wingate Expeditions of 1943 and 1944 from the Japanese Standpoint'.
[226] IWM, Misc. 54, Item 824, Field Marshal Viscount Slim to Lt. Col. H. R. K. Gibbs, Commentary notes for page 121.
[227] TNA, WO 106/4827, Symes Japanese Prisoner Interrogation, paragraph 13, p. 2.

early 1944, in mid- March, and the Symes interrogation does not at all suggest an attack was planned earlier than this. However the original plans were disrupted by Wingate and this is consistent with the more in depth American interrogations in *Japanese Monograph 134*.[228] Regarding the comments by Slim about there being only four Japanese Divisions in the whole of Burma, wasn't this effectively the reality of the strength of the Japanese assault on Arakan, Imphal & Kohima in February – March 1944? There also appears to be some personal issues between Symes and Slim that colours the latter's assessment of the interrogation.

This interrogation and report in January 1946 by Symes, is of course some -time after he was passed over for the command of Special Force in March 1944, after Wingate's death. Slim overlooked Symes, and several others, in favour of Lentaigne, a decision that led to Symes's resignation shortly afterwards. This may in turn have affected Symes's views on Slim. Might it be that Symes's interrogation report was a fair and balanced one, and unfairly dismissed by Slim? It is instructive to look into Symes's views on Wingate and Chindit operations for context.

A reading of Symes's diary of 1943-44 covering from the period of the training of Special Force in October 1943 up to and including Operation Thursday, and his resignation, shows clearly that Symes was no blind advocate nor uncritical commentator of Wingate and the Chindits. The diary entries for

---

[228] CARL, *Japanese Monograph 134, Burma Operations Record, '15th Army Operations in Imphal Area and Withdrawal to Northern Burma: Revised Edition*, (Tokyo: Headquarters United States Army, Japan Oct 1952; repr. 1957), pp. 7-9.
<http://cgsc.contentdm.oclc.org/cdm/ref/collection/p4013coll8/id/2605> [accessed 29 march 2016]

this period do demonstrate that Symes was an 'Army Establishment' man, as one would expect of a fifty year old veteran of the First World War, and one who lamented the attitude and impact of Wingate. Furthermore, he wrote very disapprovingly of Calvert on more than one occasion and was at issue with Wingate on Calvert's administrative and training capabilities. Of Wingate's return from his sickbed at the end of November to lambast the lack of progress in preparing Special Force to his satisfaction, Syme's diary entries are those of a man wrung with anxiety and embarrassment in equal measure over Wingate's behaviour and treatment of other senior officers outside of Special Force.

The standard narrative in all of the published histories of the Chindit operations describe Symes as a loyal second in command to Wingate despite the acrimonious break-up of the 70th Division he had commanded and a Division that Slim described as one of the best trained he had ever seen.[229] A cursory reading of Symes's diary suggests that such loyalty did not equate to acceptance or respect for Wingate and his closest officers. There is a notable event at the end of November 1943 when Wingate, without Symes's knowledge, went outside the usual lines of command (yet again) to castigate General Wilcox, of Central Command who had responsibility for training, supplies, rations and in particular his poorly designed training program and exercises for Special Force.

In reaction to this, regarding the insufficient ration problem with which he agreed and had himself written to Willcox about, Symes recorded on 23 November:

Wingate had sent a telegram to Army HQ about it which is very naughty, as it is going behind Willcox's back, without my knowledge, and I am responsible at the moment. Will lead to

---

[229] Slim, p. 161.

more unpleasantness with Central Command which will not improve matters. It is a strange and awkward situation with Wingate exercising control in many respects whilst not here, whilst I am supposedly in command. It makes me rather unhappy about the future.[230]

Things were no better for Symes later that week when he wrote in his diary on 27 November:

I wonder how this show is going to turn out. The inception is good – no doubt about that – but the running of it is not! […] again Calvert of 77 Bgd. is getting very much above himself. His administration is bad and in a recent letter he has been insubordinate! Later I received a letter of apology from Calvert or as near an apology he is capable of writing…

He (Wingate) was inclined to go direct to Delhi about this exercise, but I persuaded him to go and see Willcox first, at any rate. We don't want any more unpleasantness with anybody. There's been too much of that already. Later a message to say Willcox thinking it over but likely to refuse. [231]

Wingate wrote a report of his criticisms of Willcox and Central Command together with his demands to General Giffard, Commander - in - Chief 11th Army Group on 29 November, opening with:

The situation with regard to the training of the seven Brigades of the Special Force is unsatisfactory.

I am also far from satisfied as to the administrative relationship between myself and Central Command, who so far appears to have acted the part of an additional post box between ourselves and GHQ (I), thus merely delaying the

---

[230] IWM, Box No. 82/15/1, Private Papers of Major General G. W. Symes CBMC, Diary 6 November 1943 – 11th April 1944, 23 November 1943.
[231] IWM, Symes Diary, 27 November 1943.

accomplishment of mobilisation.[232]

Wingate demanded of Giffard that all training responsibility and administration of Special Force needed be given to himself. Wingate's demands were met. Writing on 30 November, Symes confided to his diary, 'It seems that Wingate has got his way & Willcox is very angry. Makes relations all the more difficult.'[233]

These exchanges are an important context in looking at the Symes Japanese Prisoner Interrogation Report and Slim's reputation and character at this time. The attitude and feelings of Symes recorded in his diary regarding Wingate and Special Force do not give the impression of a man keen to build up the posthumous reputation or potential achievements of Wingate. There is also in the diary a tantalising hint at criticism of Slim's character. There are two excerpts in particular, both related to his being passed over for command of Special Force. The first comment relates to the breaking of the news by Slim and the second in contrast to the character of General Giffard.

On first learning of his being overlooked for command of Special Force from Tulloch, on 25 March 1944 Symes wrote:

I have known and sensed that Tulloch has been in opposition to me all the time and has made no effort to keep me in the picture. Reason I don't know other than that he knows I disagree with some – or most – of the administrative methods.[234]

Symes then had a meeting with Giffard at Army HQ the next day:

There I saw Giffard who was very pleasant (he isn't a Slim) and who said that Slim wanted to put in Lentaigne, and that he,

---

[232] TNA, CAB 101/ 184, Major General Commanding Special Forces to Commander – in – Chief 11th Army Group, 'Training of Special Force', 29 January 1943.

[233]IWM, Symes Diary, 30 November 1943.

[234] IWM, Symes Diary, 25 March 1944.

Giffard, had decided to back Slim as under the circumstances he didn't think I was sufficiently in the operational picture and Slim thought Lentaigne was.[235]

The next day Symes met with Slim and the diary entry, even allowing for Symes's disappointment, suggests an underlying antagonism between the two men:

Slim sent for me at 10.30 and I thought there might be a set to and I was rather surprised when he came over all handsome, apologised for the way in which the 'news' had been conveyed to me and gave me a letter he had written to Army Group Command, explaining the circumstances, saying that he was prepared to take me on as an acting Divisional Commander, under him and so on [...] I didn't expect this but am I being very prejudiced, or is my opinion of human nature so low, when I think that having got what he wanted he can afford to go all handsome in gesture?[236]

These comments suggest that there is an underlying personal issue between Symes and Slim or perhaps Slim and Special Force, but that is not explained further by Symes. It does however create a contrast with the familiar 'Uncle Bill' image of Slim with a contrary view by a senior officer who could not be accused of being a Wingate acolyte. These last comments by Symes can be interpreted to have a meaning that goes beyond his personal disappointment and that he can see that with the appointment of Lentaigne, a fellow Gurkha officer, he 'got what he wanted', the effective control of Special Force had moved firmly to Slim.

It is also notable that Slim makes only one brief reference to Symes in *Defeat into Victory*, when 70th Division is allotted to Special Force and broken up after the Quebec Conference.

---

[235] IWM, Symes Diary, 26 March 1944.
[236] IWM, Symes Diary, 27 March 1944.

There is no mention of him thereafter, not even in his recollection of Lentaigne's appointment as Commander of Special Force. It is also notable that Symes was responsible for the LoC operations in the Fourteenth Army rear during the push through Burma in 1945 and there is likewise no mention of this in *Defeat into Victory.*

To what extent was Slim's subsequent opinions of Chindit operations clouded by his personal views and relationship with Wingate? Slim has offered that he and Wingate got on quite well on most issues and better than most people would have expected.[237] The contrary point of view is offered by Simon Anglim, in personal correspondence with the author:

Wingate's personality is undoubtedly a factor in how he is remembered. It is clear from certain letters I have read in Slim's papers at Churchill College that he and Wingate loathed each other personally, and there is at least one letter in Wingate's papers where he devotes some effort to arguing that Director Staff Duties GHQ India – S Woodburn Kirby – doesn't know what he is talking about.[238]

With this in mind might it be more than a post - war conspiracy theory of Chindit veterans that Wingate's and the Chindits' reputation was being deliberately dismantled by Slim, Kirby and their researchers?

The Barton interviews with Slim for the *Official History* paints a very jaundiced view of Wingate's qualities in describing Slim's relations with him:

In the planning stages and in the early days of the expedition he saw a lot of Wingate. Relations were not always easy. In the first place Wingate was not always to be relied upon in his

---

[237] Slim, p. 248.
[238] Dr. Simon Anglim, personal correspondence, 29 April 2016.

statements; he was, too, of a ruthless temperament, caring little for the lives or welfare of his subordinates provided he obtained what he wanted.[239]

On balance, there does appear to be a deliberate effort by Slim and other Fourteenth Army colleagues to use their positions of influence to tilt the historic record towards Slim's achievements over those of Wingate, and indeed Mountbatten. Calvert has alleged a high level conspiracy within the British Army that began in 1945 to write down the record of Wingate and the Chindits.[240] Would that really be necessary though, since Slim was CIGS by the end of 1948 and would have all the influence and authority he needed to channel the narrative which he does seem to have successfully done.

A good example of this influence by Slim is recorded in his correspondence to Kirby in researching Volume III of the *Official History*:

In general, I agree with Pownall that you have given too much space to the L.R.P. forces, giving excessive detail in both their planning and operations. This is understandable, Wingate was one of only two picturesque and puzzling figures in Burma. (Stilwell was the other) As such, quite apart from what he achieved or failed to achieve, Wingate could not fail to attract interest. However, I would suggest that in any Official History, space should be allotted according to the actual contribution to success or failure a leader or a formation made.[241]

Indeed, it is often said that the victor writes history but so too of course do the living and the survivors. Sir Robert Thompson

---

[239] TNA, CAB 106/206, Barton, Notes on Meeting with Field Marshall Slim, p. 2, para. 3, 'Relations with Wingate', 1953.
[240] Calvert, p. 259.
[241] TNA, CAB 101/185, Slim comments to Kirby, Chapter XIV, General Remarks, p. 5, 22 October 1958.

paints a vivid image of this in his autobiography when reflecting on the victory laurels awarded to Slim:

Every time I look at the picture of General Slim and his Corps Commanders being knighted by Lord Wavell as Viceroy on the field of battle after Imphal, I see the ghost of Wingate present.[242]

It seems from the evidence presented here that Slim was not misrepresented in his views of Wingate as some commentators such as Rooney have asserted, with his opinions distorted under the malign influence of Kirby and Roberts. Rather, that the Official Historian and his researchers reflected Slim's views perfectly well. In conclusion, it is clear that the views Slim had in 1956 and 1958 were consistent with those held in 1944 and he was a prime mover in the substantive reassessment of Wingate that took shape and emerged in the *Official History* and has been the main narrative to the present day.

---

[242] Thompson, p. 76.

Chapter Five: What was the measurable contribution of the Chindits to the Imphal-Kohima battles and Stilwell's advance on Myitkyina?

'We were never in contact with the Japanese, I think we were there as a form of distraction to stop the Japanese supplies going to India. We did very little fighting...'[243]

This comment made in an oral interview with Thomas Parker of 90 Column, 111th Brigade, in January 2018, is a recurring theme when dealing with the accounts of the Chindit operations, which raises real questions as to the useful extent of any military contribution that was made by those Columns not actually engaging the Japanese. Richard Rhodes James, also of 111th Brigade made a similar comment:

I remember my dismay when arriving at the lines of communication that we had travelled so far to cut and finding them little more than an overgrown track. How better could these thousands of troops have been deployed when 14th Army was in crisis?[244]

By its very nature the Long Range Penetration operations practised by Wingate and the Chindits were not the set piece battles that most soldiers and civilians alike would imagine as warfare. Slim made the same criticism of Wingate in *Defeat into Victory*:

---

[243] Oral interview with author, Private Thomas Parker, Bren Gunner, 1st Battalion, The Cameronians, 90 Column, 111th Brigade, 1944, Personal Interview, 23 January 2018, 15'00''-15'35''.

[244] Richard Rhodes James, Book Review of 'Orde Wingate and the Historians' by Peter Mead, *Journal of Southeast Asian Studies*, 19/1 (March 1988), 164-165.

As usual, I found Wingate stimulating when we talked strategy or grand tactics, but strangely naïve when it came to the business of actually fighting the Japanese. He had never experienced a real fight against them, still less a battle [...] Wingate's men were neither trained nor equipped to fight pitched battles, offensive or defensive.[245]

Slim's criticisms made in *Defeat into Victory,* were repeated in his correspondence with Kirby for Volume III of the *Official History*, covering the preparations and actions for Operation Thursday.[246]

Regarding the contribution of Special Force to the Burma campaign in these notes with Kirby, Slim is unequivocally negative:

Soberly considered, I do not believe that the contribution of Special Force was either great in effect or commensurate with the resources it absorbed, it was, I consider, surpassed by that of many of the normal divisions. Nor do I think judging by what happened when the Japanese, even with inferior forces made serious efforts against it, that Wingate's ambitious visions of his columns as the main force could ever have been translated into reality.[247]

In the context of Slim's criticisms it is important to remind ourselves of the decisions that led to the commitment of Special Force to Operation Thursday and all that followed from 16th

---

[245] Slim, *Defeat into Victory*, p. 250.

[246] TNA, CAB 101/105, Slim Correspondence with Kirby on Chapter 12 of the Official History, III, regarding Wingate's concept of warfare, 22 October 1958.

[247] TNA, CAB 101/105, Slim Correspondence with Kirby on Chapter 14 of the Official History, regarding Slim's agreement with General Pownall that too much space and attention is devoted in Volume III to Wingate and Special Force, 22 October 1958.

Brigade's march into Burma from Ledo in February, 77th Brigade's airborne assault on the night of 5-6 March and through to the evacuation of the battered and emaciated remnants of the Force from Myitkyina in August 1944. Wingate's official mission, sanctioned by a Prime Minister and a President at Quebec in August 1943 and pushed forward by the CCS, was to invade northern Burma to enable Stilwell's force of American and Chinese to advance from Ledo and capture Myitkyina. It was hoped that this would also embolden Chiang Kai –Shek to release his forces in Yunnan to advance southwards across the Salween river. In support, British IV Corps under General Scoones was to advance westwards. Slim's January 1944 instruction to Wingate restated this mission with particular emphasis on, 'Of these tasks the most important is to assist the advance of Combat Troops (Ledo Sector). [248] Ledo Force was Stilwell's force of American's (Merill's Marauders) and Chinese troops trained at Ledo under Stilwell.

Operating in advance of these Allied forces and behind the Japanese front lines was to be Wingate's Special Force. In the event, the Japanese threat and eventual invasion of India with the U-Go operation against Imphal and Kohima cancelled any westward advance by IV Corps. This emerging threat of invasion also led to Wingate evolving his LRP tactics to exploit the Japanese advance by using the space created behind their lines to create "Strongholds". These were in essence, a defensive fortification, wholly supplied by air, from which the

---

[248] TNA, WO 203/4620, Slim to Wingate, in extracts of Appendices and Annexures to Air Marshal Sir John Baldwin's Report on Operation Thursday, Annexure "A", Fourteenth Army Operation Instruction No. 51, 9 Jan 1944.

Chindit Columns could operate in lieu of any supporting advance by IV Corps, or from the Chinese under Chiang's direct control. This in turn led to Wingate developing a Plan A and a Plan B for Operation Thursday, the former following the original intent to primarily support Stilwell's mission, the latter making adaptations to additionally support the British defence of Imphal and Kohima, with the intent of attacking and hampering the rear and LoC of the invading Japanese forces.[249]

Thus, we need to make any appreciation of Chindit efforts in light of competing but interdependent missions. Firstly, the mission to assist Stilwell secure the airbase at Myitkyina, which would substantially boost the tonnage available flying the "hump", and enable the Ledo Road to link up with the northern section of the old Burma Road. This would then open up the supply route to China and fulfil the American strategic objectives to keep China in the war, commit some 700,000 Japanese troops that could otherwise be redeployed to the Pacific Theatre, and establish the VLR bomber operations against the Japanese mainland. Secondly, the Plan B mission to support the defence of Kohima and Imphal, which on the face of it was a British focused objective. However, the loss of the Imphal plain would mean the loss of supplies to Stilwell too and the rolling up of the US airfields in Assam by the Japanese.

Mountbatten's appreciation of the Special Force contribution in his post –war official report on SEAC was that:

Wingate's technique for jungle fighting with air support and supply, had suffered from certain limitations. These lightly-armed troops, divided as they were into small columns, had not been suitably equipped to undertake large-scale operations against fully organised troops; and the considerable

---

[249] TNA, AIR 23/2709, Appreciation of Situation in Northern Burma by Commander Special Force, 16 January 1944.

contribution which the Force as a whole had made to the general campaign would have been greater if it could have been made in coordination with normal formations – as in the case of 23 L.R.P. Brigade.[250]

In the absence of any advance by either the British IV Corps or the Yunnan Chinese forces, Mountbatten's comments are a factually correct assessment of the context and strategic situation to which the Chindit forces were committed to battle. This was no fault of Wingate's and both Mountbatten and Slim were always aware of such limitations of the Force when they gave Wingate his orders and committed the Chindits to Operation Thursday. It was known that the imminently expected attack on Kohima and Imphal, together with the continuing crisis in the Arakan, would forestall any such broader support. Yet the Operation did go ahead with the backing of both Mountbatten and Slim, the commanders of SEAC and Fourteenth Army. The other point made by Mountbatten is that of inadequate arms against an organised enemy. This point is aimed squarely at Stilwell, who upon taking command of the Chindits insisted on using them as assault troops against defensive positions such as Mogaung, rather than the mobile 'hit and run' tactics they were trained and equipped for.

Despite these limitations it can be argued that the contribution of the Special Force was, if not decisive, it was certainly more than negligible. Mead puts forward several examples of positive contribution:

- the diversion of Japanese air effort.
- the interruption of the supply lines of the Japanese 18th Division facing Stilwell in the north.

---

[250] Mountbatten, *Report to the Combined Chiefs of Staff*, pp. 74-75.

- 77th Brigade's capture of Mogaung and the interruption of the supply line to Mutaguchi's divisions invading Assam.[251]

Mead draws upon Japanese sources to detail the diversion of one third of the IJA's 5th Air Division in Burma against the Chindits at the same time as its 15th and 31st Divisions were launched against Imphal and Kohima.

This impact of the Chindits on the air war does deserve further detailed scrutiny beyond the immediate diversion of Japanese attention. It is arguable that a critical contribution was made by the 1st Air Commando unit attached specifically by General Arnold to the Chindits and dedicated to its operations. The first of these was in the Arakan at the battle of the Admin Box in February, prior to Operation Thursday. The light plane force of L1's and L5's that arrived in Burma with the Air Commando under Major Rebori, USAAF was split into four separate units, A-D, each providing support in different sectors, some beyond the Chindits' area of operations. Unit or "squadron" A, based at Taro in support of Ferguson and 16 Brigade; B unit based at Ledo in support of Stilwell, his Chinese forces and Merill's Marauders; C unit, supporting Calvert and 77th Brigade at Broadway; and D unit based at Ramu, in the Arakan, far from its base of operations supporting the defence of the Admin Box. The resistance of British forces here is rightly seen as a pivotal moment in the battles of 1944 which stopped the Japanese advance on India and its ultimate defeat in Burma. This resistance was greatly emboldened by the light plane force which evacuated more than seven hundred wounded and flew in replacements. A report on the light plane contribution described it as the greatest flying feat of the Arakan

---

[251] Peter Mead, p. 151.

campaign.[252] It is interesting to note that Holland's recent account of the Arakan campaign has a negligible account of the Air Commando and light plane contribution to it, following the traditional *Official History* and Slim's Fourteenth Army narrative.[253]

The other significant contribution by the Air Commandos working with Special Force was the devastating attack it made on the Japanese airfields at Shwebo and Onbauk during the initial Chindit landings at Broadway. In support of the impending attack on Imphal on 8 March, the Japanese 5th Hikoshidan had moved the 62nd, 64th and 204th Sentai forward to these airbases. The Air Commando fighter sweeps of the airfields in support of Operation Thursday caught the Japanese unaware and refuelling, resulting in 34 destroyed aircraft. The Japanese admitted the loss of 18 aircraft but whatever the results the Air Commandos had delayed the participation of the JAAF in the Imphal offensive by several days and forced the withdrawal of the 64th Sentai to Malaya to re-equip.[254]

Colonel Philip Cochrane, Co-Commander of the 1st Air Commando recounted the attack as follows:

Our vigilance paid off, and one of our flights, in always keeping a good eye on their airdromes that were there that didn't have any equipment on them, was suddenly populated with a hell of a lot of aircraft that had been sent up to start battling us. We hit them the day they landed, and they weren't well emplaced, and we burned them out on the ground. We just had a field day, and we burned everything on the ground. I don't know how many of those airplanes we got, but it was well over

---

[252] Y'Blood, pp. 79-82.
[253] James Holland, *Burma '44: The Battle That Turned Britain's War in the East* (London: Corgi, 2017).
[254] Y'Blood, p. 111.

50, 60, 80. I don't know; I forget now.[255]

Is this just the biased reminiscence of an old airman? The official British contemporary reports provide further corroboration on the impact of this action of 8-9 March 1944. Air Chief Marshall Peirse, Allied Air Commander-in-Chief, Air Command, South East Asia, writing his report to the Air Ministry in London on 10 March described the action as follows:

Result has been the most signal victory over J.A.F. in Burma ever achieved. Information from pilots' claims and subsequent reconnaissance now shows that total of forty-six aircraft were destroyed and many other damaged.[256]

The results of this attack were also detailed in the Joint Intelligence Collection Agency (JICA) report for 8 March, Mission #66, with 27 S/E Oscars destroyed on the ground, one in the air, 2 probable and 1 damaged, 6 T/E medium bombers destroyed, 1 Sally destroyed, 1 T/E transport destroyed.[257]

In a subsequent report by Peirse on 16 March the tally of Japanese aircraft destroyed is sixty-three, a consequence of further attacks on Heho, Aungban and Meiktila airfields. This report also references the success of the light plane force in the Arakan operation and in the current Operation Thursday:

Another feature of these amazing operations and one which proved so successful in the Arakan battle has been the

---

[255] USAFHRC, Colonel Philip G. Cochran, US Air Force Oral History Interview, 1975, p. 275 <http://www.afsoc.af.mil/Portals/86/documents/history/AFD-070330-008.pdf> [accessed 14 June 2017]

[256] TNA, AIR 23/7655, Operation Thursday, H.Q. Air Command SEA to Air Ministry, Whitehall, 10 March 1944, p. 2.

[257] TNA, AIR 23/1945, Joint Intelligence Collection Agency Report 1834, 15 April 1944, p. 9.

evacuation of the wounded by light aircraft. In these operations, unlike Arakan, the single engine aircraft had to fly over Burma in daylight for several hundred miles knowing full well that Jap fighters were in the neighbourhood.[258]

Is Peirse's assessment of the Air Commando led attack mere hyperbole and if not just how devastating was it? British intelligence reports from 27 January 1944 assessed the total J.A.F. strength in South East Asia (covering Burma, Siam, Malaya and Sumatra) at 333 aircraft, of which 135 were fighters. Of these enemy aircraft 198 were identified as being in the Burma theatre, of which almost all fighters were based there.[259] Therefore, the post- reconnaissance assessment of the air mission accompanying Operation Thursday is that one third of the Japanese air forces in Burma at this time were destroyed within one week. The slightly less generous assessment is that almost twenty percent of the J.A.F. in South East Asia was lost in these actions.

An even more dramatic impact of these events is evident if we look at Japanese sources of air strength in Burma. In *Japanese Monograph 64*, narrating the Japanese air campaign in Burma, the appended Map #5, on disposition of air units, lists the 5th Hikoshidan's total air strength in February 1944 at just 100 aircraft.[260]

---

[258] TNA, AIR 23/7655, Operation Thursday, H.Q. Air Command to Air Ministry, Whitehall, for Peck from Peirse, 16 March 1944, p. 5.

[259] TNA, WO 203/4620, Extracts of Appendices and Annexures to Air Marshal Sir John Baldwin's Report on Operation Thursday, Enemy Ground and Air Dispositions, Air Forces, 27 January 1944, p. 14.

[260] *Japanese Monograph 64, Record of the Air Operation in Burma Jan 1942-Aug 1945* (Tokyo: 1st Demobilization Bureau, 1946), February 1944, pp. 61-62.

Major General John Alison, USAAF, was Cochrane's Co-Commander of 1st Air Commando and made the following appreciation of the attack on Shwebo:

This one raid was probably a catastrophic blow to the Japanese Air force in Burma. When I think of what numerical losses of this kind would have done to allied forces in the area I cannot help but conclude that this raid must have broken the back of the Japanese Air Force in Burma. Although they attacked us sporadically thereafter, enemy air opposition was a negligible factor from this time on.[261]

This success was followed up in early April with an attack on Aungban airfield which resulted in the intelligence assessment of twenty-six Japanese planes destroyed, two probable and eight damaged.[262] Using the same calculation as above on the available Japanese forces, the estimation is that by 4 April forty-six percent of Japanese air resources had been destroyed in Burma and twenty-seven percent in South East Asia. These aggressive actions were primarily led by USAAF and 1st Air Commando long range P-51's and B-25's in assisting Chindit Operations 150 miles inside Japanese held Burma. Notably, the Spitfires and Hurricanes of the RAF did not have the long-range capabilities of the USAAF and 1st Air Commando in attacking the Japanese air bases.

Such losses must have been crippling to the imminent plans by the Japanese to attack Kohima and Imphal, with the SEAC forces already having wrested the balance of air superiority over

---

http://www.ibiblio.org/hyperwar/Japan/Monos/pdfs/JM-64_BurmaAirOps/JM-64_BurmaAirOps.pdf [accessed 4 September 2018]

[261] Tulloch, p. 276.

[262] TNA, AIR 23/1945, Joint Intelligence Collection Agency Report 1834, 15th April 1944, Mission #138, 4 April, 1944, p. 21.

the Japanese during the Arakan offensive in February.[263] An assessment of the Japanese counter operations over the same period illustrates how much of a destabilising factor that the Chindits must have been to Mutaguchi's offensive into Assam. Pearson, in his narrative of the air campaign in Burma comments:

5th Hikoshidan also found its objectives unexpectedly split and instead of committing its full force to the support of Fifteenth Army's assault at Imphal was required to dilute its offensive capability by attacking both IV Corps and the Chindit Operation further north.[264]

Pearson also sources the *Japanese Monograph 64*, on air operations in Burma, compiled in 1946. This details the air operations of 5th Hikoshidan between 10 March and 30 July 1944, encompassing the Chindit Operation and the Imphal assault. Of the twenty-two operations recorded up to 15 April, twelve were against Chindit forces or targets in northern Burma, not the Imphal operation.[265] This was also after the devastating attack at Shwebo by 1st Air Commandos on 8-9 March, which heavily reduced the resources of the 5th Hikoshidan. If we are to believe this contemporary record of Japanese air operations, over half of the missions in the first crucial month of the Imphal assault were diverted by the Chindit operations. Given the very close run events at Kohima and Imphal one may speculate the difference these operations might have made in edging the Japanese to their objectives had they been attacking British IV

[263] TNA, AIR 2/7990, Minute Sheet by ACSEA on Wingate's Covering Letter to Report on Air Borne Movement of Two Brigades of Special Force in Operation THURSDAY, 25 July 1944.
[264] Pearson, p. 115.
[265] Pearson, p. 176.

Corps.

Monograph 64 details that the anticipated main mission for March 1944 was the Imphal operation. It is not mere conjecture about the disruptive effects of the Chindit landings on Japanese plans. The *Japanese Monograph* states:

The main force of the 5th Air Division will cooperate with the units advancing on the ground to Imphal. After the end of the joint operation in the Akyab area, we will postpone the joint operation in order to advance to Imphal, so that the air unit may prepare for the next operation.[266]

Also attached to the invading Japanese infantry were the airfield company to make ready captured Allied airfields and the air and ground communication company advanced in anticipation of the combined air ground assault on Imphal.[267] We can see from this Japanese source that the air component of the U-Go offensive was well-planned and an integral part of both the Imphal invasion and subsequent planned exploitation of Allied bases.

Despite such plans, for two weeks at the outset of the invasion, the J.A.F. support of the infantry was negligible and this is evident in the mission records. The J.A.F. was focused on the Chindit threat and at the same time was heavily depleted by the aggressive long range air missions supporting Wingate's force. The three Sentai assembling at Shwebo on 8 March would have numbered eighty-one aircraft that were diverted from the Imphal offensive – in fact they barely got off the ground. Given the close run defence of Imphal and Kohima it is surely an injustice to Wingate's memory to dismiss the Chindit contribution as Giffard and Slim did. Without Operation Thursday Slim may never have had the opportunity to spring

---

[266] *Monograph 64*, p. 59.
[267] *Monograph 64*, p. 60.

the trap on Mutaguchi that he so elaborately describes in *Defeat into Victory*.

The post operational report by 77th Brigade made the following observations on the impact of air superiority and close air support:

The lowest private in the Imperial Japanese Army considers himself invincible on the ground, and there is no doubt that he is an exceptional soldier. But at the back of his mind there is a steadily growing fear of the air. The scarcity of his own and the superfluity of Allied aircraft keep driving this home. He expects in the end to be defeated by air strategy and air operations beyond his imagination.[268]

If this was the effect on Japanese troops 150 miles inside their front line how much more acute must it have been for those under almost unfettered attack from the air at Imphal and Kohima? This air dominance was in large part a consequence of the aggressive air support of Operation Thursday.

It is also necessary to challenge Slim's repeated criticisms of Special Force not delivering the returns commensurate with the resources deployed. Is Slim looking at the balance of the scales in relation to the defence of Kohima and Imphal for which even he acknowledged in his orders to Wingate was not the objective? Any serious assessment of the Chindit contribution must look at the Burma theatre as a whole, as part of the CBI theatre, its relation to the American Pacific theatre, and of course to the global Alliance and the Germany first strategy being pursued in Europe. The Chindits were not deployed in Operation Thursday to primarily assist the defence of India but to fulfil Britain's wider commitments to its main ally.

---

[268] TNA, WO 203/1829, 77 Indian Infantry Brigade of 3rd Indian Division, Operations in Burma, February – August 1944.

The enduring commitment since August 1943 was to assist Stilwell in northern Burma to secure the air and land routes to China. That this was the main mission is often forgotten by British commentators and critics of Wingate and partly due to Wingate's own making in his enthusiasm for both the A and B plans.

The recap, the A Plan was the assistance of Stilwell in the cutting of the lines of communications in the north to Japanese 18th Division and the B Plan the exploitation of extended lines of communication in the west to the Japanese 15th, 31st and 33rd Divisions, taking part in Mutaguchi's invasion of Assam. The success of the Chindits in supporting Stilwell in achieving his objectives is almost lost in any historical appreciation of the campaign, overshadowed as they are by the controversies surrounding the personalities and actions of Stilwell and especially Major General Lentaigne, who succeeded Wingate after his death in a plane crash on 24 March. At the conclusion of the Chindit operations Lentaigne made the following comments at a press conference:

Well, the plan succeeded, there is no doubt about it because Gen. Stilwell got his objectives of Mogaung and Myitkyina, and we blocked the road and railway permanently for about 3 out of 5 months, and the remaining 2 months there were columns operating against the railway from either flank, which kept the Jap frightened to use large scale train movement or to use M.T. in any large scale on the road which runs up the valley by the railway.[269]

In the round Lentaigne was correct. However, the period of Lentaigne's leadership was mired in controversy at the time and remains a key theme of the Chindit issue regarding its efficacy,

---

[269] TNA, WO 203/4620, Lentaigne Press Conference Transcript, undated 1944, p. 2.

especially after Slim wholly assigned it to Stilwell's command. The comments made by Lentaigne were also supported by Slim in the notes of one of his interviews for the *Official History* in 1953, although still doubting the overall balance of contribution:

In Field Marshal Slim's opinion the Second Chindit Expedition did not bring in as big a military return as was hoped, for the amount of resources used. Nevertheless, it did greatly back General Stilwell to capture Mogaung and Myitkyina, it inflicted quite a considerable number of casualties on the Japanese, and it made the enemy L. of C. to the west more difficult to maintain.[270]

This comment by Slim, several years before *Defeat into Victory* was published, suggests that the Chindits were having some success in pursuing both Plan A, the assistance of Stilwell, and Plan B, the assistance of Fourteenth Army. These two objectives were both competing and complementary since the loss of Assam would cut off Stilwell's supply lines and leave him isolated while at the same time Stilwell would have been opposed to a reassignment of Special Force which would relieve pressure on the Japanese lines of communication to its 18th Division facing him.

Tulloch identifies the decisions over these two plans as the crux of the arguments in his book and that Slim's decision to commit the Chindits to Plan A was the main reason for the heavy losses that subsequently resulted. Tulloch attributes ninety percent of the Chindit casualties to this fateful decision. [271] He describes being consulted by Slim on the possibility of

---

[270] TNA, CAB 106/206, Notes on Meeting with Field Marshall Slim with Corrections by Slim, Results of Chindit Effort in 1944, 2 April 1953, p. 6.
[271] Tulloch, p. 239.

disengaging the Chindit forces from Stilwell's front and concentrating them across the Chindwin to the west in support of the besieged IV Corps. Despite the ultimate decision to fully commit to Plan A, Tulloch is in no doubt that at the end of March 1944 Wingate's Plan B was already successfully directed towards blocking communications to all the Japanese divisions facing IV Corps, with Slim's knowledge and consent. His evidence for this is the testimony of General Kawabe, in *Japanese Monograph 134*.[272]

Kawabe's testimony details a number of consequences that befell the Japanese invading forces as a direct consequence of Wingate's Special Force deployment:

1. 15th Army's timetable was severely disrupted affecting its operations and eventually led to the abandonment of northern Burma.

2. 15th Army H.Q. was delayed from advancing to Imphal until late April, leading to inadequate liaison with the divisions involved in the Imphal operation and alienating divisional commanders from Army H.Q.

3. The lines of communication to 15th and 31st Divisions was cut off and the planned transfer of vehicles from Indaw-Homalin area south to Shwebo –Kelewa road was prevented.

4. Elements of 15th Division were diverted to combat the Chindit threat and 53rd Division, the only reserve available to the Area Army could not be deployed as a strategic reserve for the Imphal Operation.

5. The 5th Air Division was committed to a large extent to combat the Wingate force and could render little assistance to the Imphal Operation.

6. The supply route to 18th Division was cut off when it was already committed to heavy fighting in the Huwkawng area.

---

[272] Tulloch, p. 238.

7. The unauthorised withdrawal of 31st Division by its commander was a consequence of 15th Army's failure to provide his division with supplies.

8. 31st Division's withdrawal destroyed all hope of taking Imphal and made vulnerable the position of 15th Division.

9. The collapse of the 31st Division, the advent of the rainy season and the suspension of the flow of military supplies forced the 15th Army to abandon all hope of recovering from the disastrous situation. [273]

This powerful testimony by the Japanese officers in Burma was given little credence by both the *Official History* and by Slim. Yet Tulloch raises a very key question about Slim's decision to wholly allocate Special Force to Stilwell, under the American's command and in a role they were neither equipped nor trained for as conventional infantry without the supporting firepower. If *Monograph 134* was the professional opinion of the Japanese officers as to the effect of Special Force on the Imphal Operation, how much more impactful might it have been had Plan B been adopted completely? It is arguable that the Japanese collapse would have been both more rapid and complete rather than the uncertain outcome that persisted through April – June 1944.

As Tulloch comments on the transfer of Special Force to Stilwell on 9th April:

Under Stilwell, all the ground held by Special Force was given up. Aberdeen and Broadway were closed after fulfilling

---

[273] CARL, *Japanese Monograph 134, Burma Operations Record, 15th Army Operations in Imphal Area and Withdrawal to Northern Burma* (Tokyo: Headquarters United States Army, Japan Oct 1952; repr, 1957), pp. 149-155.
<http://cgsc.contentdm.oclc.org/cdm/ref/collection/p4013coll8/id/2605> [accessed 29 march 2016]

all that Wingate had hoped for in his stronghold theories [...] The morale of the Special Force brigades, already undermined by Wingate's death, had received a bitter blow by the decision to move north. To the men their successes were now being surrendered for the uninspiring task of helping Stilwell achieve objectives which, in their view, he should have achieved by the end of April (Mogaung in particular).[274]

Further context to *Japanese Monograph 134* is given in *Japanese Monograph 45*, which deals with the broad sweep of Japanese strategy across all theatres 1941-45. Regarding the U-GO Operation to invade Assam, the Army General Staff put several key questions and concerns to Mutaguchi prior to approving the operation:

1. Could the Southern Army deal successfully with an Allied seaborne attack from the Bay of Bengal during the operation?

2. Could Burma be defended successfully if the front was extended into Assam?

3. Could the small J.A.F. keep pace with the ground forces and support them throughout the operation?

4. Was the supply position satisfactory?

5. Could 15th Army's plan be relied upon?[275]

The first concern wouldn't be an issue since the British couldn't raise sufficient amphibious and naval forces due to the

---

[274] Tulloch, pp. 247-48.

[275] CARL, *Japanese Monograph 45, History of Imperial General Headquarters, Army Section* (Tokyo: Headquarters United States Army, Japan, 1952; repr. 1959), pp. 161-62.

<http://cgsc.contentdm.oclc.org/cdm/ref/collection/p4013coll8/id/2475> [accessed 29 March 2016]

prioritisation of Germany and the planned cross-Channel operations in Normandy.

The second concern was borne out by the rapid collapse of the Japanese position in northern Burma during the desperate retreat from Assam. This collapse was due to the unexpected resistance of the Allied forces at Kohima and on the Imphal plain but also because the third and fourth concerns of the General Staff were quite prescient. The J.A.F. was both crippled and diverted by the Chindit operation and the supply position was made critical by the constriction and destruction of its lines of communication. With these factors working against the invasion, 15th Army's plan did indeed become unreliable.

It is stated by Bidwell, amongst other British commentators, that Mutaguchi's forces attacked with just three weeks supplies in hand, secure in their assumptions of British retreat and surrender of the bountiful supplies at Dimapur.[276] This may in itself be a fair description of the prevailing attitude of Mutaguchi and the Japanese but this does not invalidate the physical lines of communication preparation and planning of the U-GO operation, and the impact on these of the subsequent destruction of huge supply dumps by the Chindits and 1st Air Commando east of Indaw. This contributed to the virtual mutiny of 31st Division because its supplies were not getting through, which according to *Japanese Monograph 134* led to the unhinging of the whole plan. Bidwell goes to some length to dismiss the impact on the Japanese supplies based on conjecture on quantities destroyed and probable requirements. This argument doesn't take into account the physical constriction of the supply route which the Chindits achieved by virtue of being astride the railway between Indaw and Myitkyina in combination with the constant air action in further

---

[276] Bidwell, pp. 171-74.

indicting Japanese movement.

Bidwell argues that the stopping of the initial assault was critical and in this the Chindits were not yet in place to have a critical impact:

Nor was the supply factor the decisive one. The Kohima garrison held on after a heroic defence until April 5th [...] But the 14th Chindit Brigade was not able to begin full-scale operations against the Japanese 31st Division until mid-April.[277]

To counter this there is an appreciation written by Wingate to Slim on 21 March, just days before his death, on the opportunity to exploit his Plan B. This appreciation acknowledges the time factor and necessary defence required by IV Corps in the meantime:

If, however, in the future, the troops deployed under 4th Corps succeed in putting up a stout resistance, then the Japanese will be compelled to bring up large quantities of ammunition and other stores to <u>maintain</u> their offensive. In doing so they are compelled to use the roads, very carefully prepared for over 18 months. Even allowing for the Japanese superiority to ourselves in this respect, without proper communications they cannot drift at will over precipitous and barren regions. Their routes are perfectly well known to us.[278]

The emphasis on the word 'maintain' has been added by this author to clearly flag the fact that Wingate is not proposing that the Chindit force will successfully defeat the attacks on Kohima and Imphal, but he is proposing to materially assist in the subsequent exploitation of a successful defence and destruction of the Japanese forces. The *Japanese Monograph* testimony

---

[277] Bidwell, p. 173.
[278] TNA, CAB 101/184, Extracts from Wingate Papers, Appreciation of situation in Northern Burma by Commander, Special Force for Commander 14th Army, 21 March 1944.

suggests that this was indeed the case.

Wingate initiated his plan B on 22 March when 14th Brigade was flown into the Aberdeen airstrip. After a lengthy deployment due to transport shortages as a result of the emergency at Imphal, it operated south-west of Indaw, to block Japanese reinforcements moving up to challenge 77th Brigade at White City. 14th Brigade also attacked supply dumps and railway targets. 111th Brigade initially took over 14th Brigade's original task under plan A to indict east- west communications, but was later switched to attacking the Japanese supply dumps west of Indaw. Wingate's orders to 14th Brigade were to interrupt communications in the Pinlebu area to force the withdrawal of Japanese 31st and 15th Divisions. The Pyingaing communications were also to be attacked, which was a bottleneck through which Japanese 33rd Division LoC passed.[279]

The status of the Chindit Brigades at the end of March 1944 as recounted by Tulloch was as follows:

- 77th Brigade was firmly lodged at the Broadway landing strip, dominating the area and had halted Japanese river traffic on the Irrawaddy. A strong block had also been made near Mawlu (White City) astride the rail and road LoC of Japanese 18th Division. This action was in direct support of Stilwell and consistent with Plan A. The block remained in place for a crucial eight weeks until 8 May when Lentaigne ordered it abandoned.

- Morris Force was operating hit and run raids on the Lashio - Myitkyina LoC of 56th Division before moving north to join Dah force which was in some disarray after a night attack at Nahpaw.

---

[279] Tulloch, p. 227.

- 111ᵗʰ Brigade were concentrating to block the Pinlebu – Pinbon LoC of 15ᵗʰ Division.

- Bladet Force, a small detachment under Major Blain, had successfully blown a railway bridge south of Wuntho.

- 14ᵗʰ Brigade while still in the process of flying in were blocking the Indaw - Banmauk road and also concentrating in the Meza railway station area to block the southern approaches to Indaw and White City.

- 16ᵗʰ Brigade had failed in its objective of seizing Indaw, after a long march southwards from Ledo that started in mid-February, but was now concentrating at the Aberdeen stronghold. From here the Indaw-Banmauk road had been blocked and enemy supply columns ambushed.

- 3ʳᵈ West African Brigade after some initial setbacks from a Japanese surprise attack was deploying to both Aberdeen and White City for garrison duties.

- 23ʳᵈ Brigade was held in reserve in Assam at Slim's insistence and was never deployed but did operate magnificently in the defence of Kohima operating as a short range penetration force outflanking and harrying Japanese formations.

Tulloch was of the belief that at this point both Plan A and Plan B could have been successfully executed.[280] This required the release of 23ʳᵈ Brigade to operate to the south to block Japanese 31ˢᵗ Division's L of C, which was Wingate's intention. Plan A's successful conclusion required Stilwell to attack Mogaung, as was the understood and agreed plan. He didn't, he

---

[280] Tulloch, pp. 244-246.

attempted to seize Myitkyina without informing SEAC, leaving the Chindit forces to evacuate their positions and move north to fill the vacuum. The other crucial factor according to Tulloch was that Chiang Kai-Shek had refused his permission for the Chinese under Stilwell to advance on Kamaing, when ordered to do so on 20 March and 4 April. They finally did so on 19 May, Kamaing fell on 16 June and Mogaung was also reached. Had this occurred when originally ordered 77th Brigade would have still invested White City and 14th and 16th Brigades would have continued the destruction of supply dumps and airfield facilities around Indaw that they had been doing successfully from 15-30 April.[281]

After Wingate's death on 24 March, he was replaced by Major General Lentaigne on 27 March, who had been GOC of 111th Brigade. Much of the criticism from Chindit commentators of operations mainly refer to this leadership under Lentaigne as one of indecision and poor decisions, such as the abandonment of White City and Broadway on 9-10 May, and the establishment of a new stronghold, Blackpool, in a less than ideal location on the 7-8 May. Initially, Wingate's plan B was endorsed by Mountbatten at a commander's conference at Jorhat on 3 April, which included Slim and Stilwell. This saw the allocation of both 14th and 111th Brigades to operate against Japanese Fifteenth Army communications. However, as mentioned earlier, 23rd Brigade was switched to a short range penetration role near Kohima.

The commitment to Plan B was abandoned within a week. Slim's concerns over the defence of Assam precluded any relieving garrison force being flown in to Indaw to exploit the position established by the Chindits and it seemed logical from his position to release the Brigades northwards to assist Stilwell

---

[281] Tulloch, p. 247.

more directly. This was in accordance with the original Wingate mission agreed at Quebec, the plan A, and although Tulloch was critical as he advocated plan B, Calvert, in charge of 77th Brigade always favoured plan A.[282] At the end of April, 16th Brigade was flown out of the Aberdeen and White City strongholds after securing Indaw airfield with 14th Brigade and destroying Japanese supplies. A week later White City was abandoned too and the artillery used in its defence flown back to Assam, as was also the case with the close down of Aberdeen. The Chindit infantry columns all headed north to establish or assist Blackpool and 111th Brigade.

The monsoon had now started in earnest and both 14th and 77th Brigades couldn't reach Blackpool with swollen rivers and chaungs cutting them off. Lengtaigne was now under pressure from Stilwell to support his command more directly. In response, Slim officially handed over control of the Chindits to Stilwell on 16-17 May. A week later Blackpool was abandoned and 111th and 3rd West African Brigades headed north to Indawgyi Lake. At this point all of the Chindit Brigades anticipated and expected to be withdrawn but Stilwell insisted on continued attacks on 18th Division rear positions and supplies. According to most histories this was a period of scandalous misuse and wastage of the Chindit force with head - on attacks required by a force ill-equipped or trained to do so, most famously at Mogaung on June 26 after three weeks bitter fighting by 77th Brigade. The dwindling Chindit forces of 77th, 14th and 3rd West African Brigades was finally withdrawn to India on 27th August.

This lengthy narrative on the Chindit operations from late March – August 1944 is important because the different phases of the campaign must be distinguished when making

---

[282] Tulloch, p. 243.

judgements on its effectiveness. At the conclusion of Chindit operations the losses were 3,628 killed, wounded and missing across the five brigades which was about twenty percent.[283] Of these losses almost ninety percent were attributable to the period under Stilwell's command.[284]

Tulloch states that Slim believed in hindsight that it was a mistake not to adopt the plan B.[285] The evidence of this is in Slim's *Defeat into Victory*:

Imphal was the decisive battle; it was there only that vital injury could be inflicted on the Japanese Army, and I should have concentrated all available forces to that end. I fear I fell into the error of so many Japanese, and persisted in a plan which should have been changed.[286]

Calvert, in command of 77th Brigade details that between 6 March and 2 May, before Wingate's simultaneous plans were abandoned and 16th Brigade were flown out, that 20,000 Chindits defeated or partially destroyed 14 ½ Japanese battalions, in engagements at Broadway, White City, Indaw and the Bhamo-Myitkyina Road.[287] A Japanese battalion was typically assessed at approximately 1,100 men, at full strength, by US Army estimates. Therefore, prior to the switch to Stilwell, Japanese formations of up to 15,950 men were defeated by Chindit forces, or even at half strength, approximately 8,000. Calvert goes on to detail the actions after 2 May when the Chindits helped destroy 53rd Japanese Division, moved into Burma as Mutaguchi's reserve for the Assam assault. The destruction at Mogaung of 128th Regiment, 1st

---

[283] Tulloch, p. 353.

[284] Tulloch, p. 239.

[285] Tulloch, p. 238.

[286] Slim, p. 307.

[287] Calvert, pp. 256-57.

Battalion, 151st Regiment and 1st Artillery Regiment would account by the same reckoning for between 3,000 - 6,000 Japanese. The remainder of 53rd Division, approximately 10-12,000 men, were diverted away from Impahal-Kohima to chase Chindits.

In summary, we can therefore calculate that Special Force operations occupied, reduced or destroyed Japanese ground forces numbering some 30,000 men, optimistically, and perhaps 15,000 at the lower end estimate. At this point there is a complete and illogical disconnect with the assertions of Kirby's *Official History*. In the Retrospect section that concludes *Volume III*, Kirby states that:

Moreover, it must be remembered that, throughout the whole period it was operating in Burma, Special Force never contained more than about two-fifths of its own strength.[288]

In riposte to Kirby's assertion that only 8,000 Japanese were contained by the Chindit forces, Calvert's penultimate page in his account of the Chindit battles is worthy of an extended quotation:

So the eventual victory at Imphal / Kohima was won by the equivalent of 8 and 2/3 British / Indian infantry divisions supported by good armour and heavy artillery with overwhelming air superiority, against three undoubtedly excellent Japanese Divisions with a few obsolete tanks, mainly pack artillery, completely inadequate air support, operating in unfriendly country at least one hundred miles from their bases (some of which had been destroyed by the Chindits) [...] Yet the Chindits, only about the equivalent of two light divisions with little artillery, destroyed the equivalent of one Japanese division and helped to divert and destroy another (the 53rd) although they were operating amidst the Japanese

---

[288] Kirby, III, p. 445.

communications and close to the Jap supplies.[289]

Ultimately, when assessing the efficacy of the Chindit operations with the hindsight of the eventual victory over the Japanese in Burma we should remember the lengths to which the British forces went to avoid battle in the years, months and weeks prior to Mutaguchi's attack on Assam. Even as Ferguson's 16th Brigade made its arduous six- hundred mile trek southward from Ledo it was the Supreme Allied Commander, Mountbatten, who initiated the Axiom mission to London and Washington to cancel ground operations in Burma in favour of combined amphibious operations bypassing Burma, when resources allowed. With Stilwell also committed to his advance from the north towards Mogaung and Myitkyina it took Roosevelt's note to Churchill on 25 February to remind the British of their prior commitments to Allied strategy.

Wingate made the point effectively in his forceful and somewhat disgusted admonishment of 11 Army Group and Fourteenth Army strategy when arguing with Slim for additional support:

The Americans are fighting in north Burma and are anxious that we should too. The projected L.R.P. operation is one of great promise. To call it off will be to disgrace us in the eyes of our allies. At the same time to stage it with no support whatever from the main British forces is to court disaster.[290]

After the spectacular successes of 1st Air Commando in support of Wingate's Special Force in the invasion of Burma, and as the battles still raged at Kohima and Imphal, Colonel Cochran returned to Washington in late May 1944. There he

---

[289] Calvert, p. 259.

[290] TNA, CAB 101/184, Statement made by Commander Special Forces at HQ 14th Army on 25 January 1944, Summing Up, p. 3.

was asked by General Arnold about the wisdom of sending more Air Commandos to Burma. Cochran advised against it as he had little faith in the British to prosecute the war with the additional resources. Cochran records that he told Arnold:

'No, it's a kind of waste'. I described some of the attitudes, and I remember being asked about the British effort out there, and how kind of complacent it was, and not terribly aggressive [...] But the British Army out there was full of that kind of thing, and the Air Force – it was obvious.[291]

Arnold was probably seeking affirmation of what he had been told earlier by Cochran's co-commander, Alison, on his return to Washington in April:

According to Alison, the general told him, 'This has been such a success. I have given authorization to form four more Air Commando groups and the necessary transport. I have already implemented the organization of two of them.'

'General, what are they going to do?' Alison replied.

'We are going to retake Burma from the air'.

'Whose troops are we going to use?' a sceptical Alison asked.

Arnold said, 'We are going to move the British Army into Burma.'

This was too much for Alison, who blurted, 'General, I don't think the British Army is going into Burma.'[292]

Without denigrating the huge achievements of Fourteenth Army in the battles of the Arakan, Imphal and Kohima and the sweeping successes that followed in late 1944, it was not British policy to go for an all-out attack in Burma and it was certainly not that of the SACSEA, Mountbatten. Might it be that Slim, secure in his success and recognition by the 1950's, shaped the narrative, together with Kirby and others as willing agents, to

---

[291] Cochrane, Interview, pp. 369-70.
[292] Y'Blood, p. 123.

position Fourteenth Army's success as something more elaborate than the opportunistic exploitation of what was a catastrophic error of judgement by Mutaguchi? An error aided in large part by Wingate in his two operations of 1943 and 1944, and by Stilwell and the USAAF resources that delivered the means, by airpower and air supply.

Chapter Six: Conclusions
Wingate and the Chindits: A Balanced Perspective in Summary

Louis Allen wrote that the Burma Campaign needed Wingate, for all his faults and inadequacies, to enliven the British efforts in this theatre.[293] The same should be said of the Anglo - American Alliance, it needed Wingate, who provided a timely catalyst for agreement between the Allies at Quebec. Continued inactivity in Burma would not be countenanced by the Americans on the excuse of resources being needed for Overlord. As Brower concludes of the Quadrant strategy for the Americans, they required action in northern Burma to pursue their China policy and a firm commitment for Overlord.[294] Northern Burma didn't require amphibious resources and the British hoped that Wingate offered a low intensity alternative to the outright invasion of Burma, Wingate was a compromise solution that suited both parties.

In any re-evaluation of Wingate it must be stressed that Slim's reputation and legacy are not in any doubt. He is rightly lauded as one of Britain's greatest generals. In the immediate post war years though, his public reputation and recognition was not nearly so well regarded outside of Fourteenth Army. Unfortunately, the measures to establish this reputation by Slim and the Official Historians and their researchers, did indeed denigrate Wingate's reputation and legacy. That denigration persists to this day.

There can be no quarrel that Wingate was a difficult character

---

[293] Allen, p. 116.
[294] Brower, pp. 56-57.

who made many enemies on his own side in his zeal to fight the Japanese. His lack of respect for the chain of command and his narrow, single-minded vision of purpose was well summed up by Mountbatten, who described him as making enemies of those best disposed towards helping him, 'Your astounding telegram to Joubert has made me realise how you have achieved such amazing success in getting yourself disliked by people who are only too ready to be on your side'[295]

However, that his peculiar character and personality and the friction it caused with Fourteenth Army should be the defining image of the Chindits and their contribution to the Burma Campaign and beyond, is disingenuous to both the man and those that fought with him. The most puzzling aspect of researching this book was the highly contrasting assessments of Wingate and the Chindits between the British and American sources. The British literature and historiography revolves around Slim and the one-eyed *Official History* appreciation of Wingate's perceived personal and professional inadequacies.

By stark contrast, the American perspective is generally rooted in the military rather than a personal appreciation of Wingate and the decisions taken in 1943 to support him, together with the diverging British and American objectives in Burma. In order to understand this dichotomy of views it is necessary to look at the Chindit campaign as both a fully combined arms and an Allied operation, with Special Force and 1st Air Commando being two parts of the same whole. Slim takes a literary swipe at this fact in *Defeat into Victory*, when commenting negatively on private armies and private air forces.[296] In contrast, the American perspective generally

[295] Philip Ziegler, *Mountbatten: The Official Biography* (London: Book Club Associates, 1985), p. 276.
[296] Slim, pp. 625-27.

celebrates the innovation of the close air support and air supply that 1st Air Commando gave to the Chindits, an innovative experiment that no lesser men than General Arnold and General Marshall of the US JCS fully endorsed and personally backed. It is instructive to remember that Marshall was the Allied general *primus inter pares* of both the US Joint Chiefs of Staff and the Allied Combined Chiefs of Staff. Any full and rounded appreciation of Wingate must be in the wider context of the exigencies and challenges of the Anglo-American Alliance in 1943-44.

The US war colleges have numerous theses that look at the inspiration of this combined force in terms of its lessons and legacy through to Vietnam and the present day requirements for unconventional arms and tactics. Thus, the perspective is one of innovation of tactics and strategy rather than personality. Of the British sources only a recent writer and student of Wingate, Simon Anglim, seems to take the same long- term appreciation as the American sources, although many writers have fought against the Slim and *Official History* versions of the Chindit operations.

Of these writers, Peter Mead made a very prescient comment on the *Official History*:

Authors and historians have frequent recourse to them, to spare themselves the time and effort of original research [...] official histories often give the clearest and most balanced view of the plans and operations described; they are almost invariably accepted as accurate, and usually they *are* accurate. When, however, they are inaccurate or prejudiced in some way, such inaccuracy and prejudice tends to spread unchecked and to be extremely hard to counter. So it has proved with the *Official History's* treatment of Orde Wingate.[297]

---

[297] Mead, p. 18.

Since Mead wrote these words in 1987, popular histories of the Burma campaign and biographies of Slim have been written by various authors giving the same biased view of Wingate as a mentally unbalanced and over promoted egotist.[298] The list of books is surprisingly extensive and all this despite the efforts of former Chindits like Peter Mead, and Tulloch, Calvert and Sir Robert Thompson before him, to counter this view. In discussing this present study with a fellow military historian, he offered the point of view to the author, that surely the history of the Chindits and Wingate had been redressed in recent years and there was nothing to prove. On the contrary, the numerous popular history books written in the last decade would suggest this is not the case at all.

Amongst the anti- Wingate authors aforementioned, Callaghan correctly identifies the context of the strategic needs

---

[298] Max Hastings, *Nemesis: The Battle for Japan, 1944-45* (London: Harper Press, 2007; repr. 2014); *Finest Years: Churchill as Warlord 1940-45* (London: Harper Press, 2009); Robert Lyman, *Slim, Master of War: Burma, 1942-5: Burma and the Birth of Modern Warfare* (London: Constable & Robinson, 2004); Frank McLynn, *The Burma Campaign: Disaster into Triumph 1942-45* (London: Random House, 2011); Russell Miller, *Uncle Bill: The Authorised Biography of Field Marshal Viscount Slim* (London: Weidenfeld & Nicolson, 2013); Julian Thompson, *The Imperial War Museum Book of War Behind Enemy Lines* (London: Sidgwick & Jackson, 1998; repr. 1999); *The Imperial War Museum Book of the War in Burma 1942-1945* (London: Pan 2002); *Forgotten Voices of Burma* (London: Ebury Press, 2009); Dr. Raymond Callahan, 'The Strange Case of the Prime Minister and the Fighting Prophet', The Churchill Centre, *Finest Hour*, 139 (Summer 2008), 36-39.
<http://www.winstonchurchill.org/publications/finest-hour/finest-hour-139> [accessed 21 May 2016]

of the Alliance but perpetuates the negative myths. Callaghan wrote:

The Wingate ploy did turn aside for a time American pressure over Burma. By the time the fallacy in long range penetration tactics was clear, China fever had somewhat abated in Washington. Whatever may be made of Wingate and his ideas—and most historians now regard him as a long and contentious footnote to the Burma campaign—Churchill scored a considerable success in alliance politics at Quebec. If the price of this success was to complicate vastly the life of the India Command, one suspects that would have bothered him very little.[299]

The fact that Wingate openly criticised his own military for a lack of proactive attitude in Burma was well-received by the Americans who widely shared this view of the British and saw Wingate as the best bet for getting something done in pursuit of their own strategy in Burma and especially China.

The Burma narrative has become the familiar British Fourteenth Army narrative of Slim, *Defeat into Victory* and the *Official History*. Yet the great achievements of Slim and Fourteenth Army were made in the last ten months of the Burma campaign and conveniently glosses over the fierce debates and disagreements between the Allies up to the tipping point of Mutaguchi's failed gamble in Assam in March - July 1944. For more than two years, from January 1942 - February 1944 the British contribution to the Allied cause in CBI had been one of defeats, disappointments and dissembling over potential operations.

From an American perspective the pressing need was to support Chiang, and keep China in the war. Their only leverage was through British agency, as Brower so clearly traces, with

---

[299] Callahan, p. 39.

its armed forces and air bases in India and at the Burmese border in Assam. Perhaps Wingate's greatest fault in the eyes of the British establishment was that he clove to the mission assigned to him at Quebec too eagerly and for too long and too readily to serving the American interpretation of warfare in Burma against the Japanese.

In conclusion, this book set out to assess several propositions related to the Chindit contribution to the Burma campaign. It is this author's opinion from reviewing the evidence that:

1. The Chindits were indeed an expedient but important bargaining chip within the global strategic context of Grand Alliance politics as expressed in the China-Burma-India theatre. Unfortunately many British perspectives critical of Wingate fail to recognise the importance of this aspect of the Chindit contribution to Allied compromise over strategy in Burma and beyond.

2. The motives of the US and Britain did differ quite markedly and Wingate's ideas allowed the Allies to reconcile these differences by using the Chindit force primarily in support of American political and military objectives within a predominantly British theatre of war.

3. Operation Longcloth and its propaganda management was vitally important in shaping the expectations of the British and Americans in the lead up to the Quebec agreement on the Burma strategy. It wasn't simply an ineffectual raid, it reinvigorated British morale and American resolve to see the British commit to offensive action.

4. American support of the Chindits from the direct and contingent contribution of 1st Air Commando was very significant in attaining air superiority in Burma.

In two individual actions alone, in support of Operation Thursday, the Air Commando struck crippling blows to the IJAAF.

5. The Air Commando came with the condition that it was reserved for supporting Wingate's operations. The American sources of Pogue, Marshall's biographer, and Cochrane's post –war interviews are categorical about this.

6. This American support was key to the development of air-land battle tactics, lines of communications and air supply that were so crucial to the eventual Burma victory. The majority of cargo planes were American. The majority of long-range fighters and fighter bombers were American. Without Wingate less of these assets would have been made available.

7. It does appear that for Slim, it was as much a personal as it was a purely military assessment of Wingate that led to his negative judgement of the Chindits' contribution relative to the resources expended. There was a consistency in his views that pre –dates both *Defeat into Victory* and the *Official History*, and despite eulogies uttered upon Wingate's death in 1944, he didn't think much of the man or his ideas.

8. The measurable impact and contribution of the Chindits to the Imphal-Kohima battles and Stillwell's advance on Myitkyina suggests that Calvert has a very good question about the treatment of the Chindits in the Official History and by Slim.

The last words should go to Brigadier Michael Calvert, who always remained loyal to Wingate, and whose fighting credentials were impeccable. He concluded his *Prisoners of Hope*, with the following:

But the fact remains that Wingate and the Chindits undoubtedly had a decisive effect on the war in Burma in 1944 by breaching the wall of mountains around Burma, preventing the Japanese from using interior lines to defeat each threat (British, American, Chinese) in turn and letting in the Allies from the north on to the Burma plain behind the Japanese facing Fourteenth Army. Yet neither Wingate nor the Chindits have been given their military due for their sacrifices and tactical and strategical successes.[300]

---

[300] Calvert, p. 260.

Appendices

Appendix A
Operation Longcloth[301]
February - June 1943

Order of Battle: 77th Indian Infantry Brigade
Commander: Major General O. C. Wingate, DSO

No.1 Group (Southern)
Lieutenant-Colonel Alexander, 3/2nd Gurkha Rifles (2GR)

Major G. Dunlop, MC, Royal Scots   : 1 Column
Major A. Emmet, 3/2nd Gurkha Rifles (2GR): 2 Column

No.2 Group (Northern)
Lieutenant-Colonel S.A. Cooke, The Lincolnshire Regiment (attached, The King's (Liverpool) Regiment) (King's)
   Major J.M. Calvert, Royal Engineers (RE): 3 Column
   Major Conron, 3/2nd Gurkha Rifles (2GR): 4 Column
   (Later, Major R.B.G. Bromhead, Royal Berkshire Regiment)
   Major B.E. Ferguson, The Black Watch (BW): 5 Column
   Major K.D. Gilkes, The Kings (Liverpool) Regiment (King's): 7 Column
   Major WP Scott, The Kings (Liverpool) Regiment (King's):8 Column

---

[301] Tony Redding, *War in the Wilderness* (Stroud, The History Press, 2011) p. 45.

No. 6 Column was broken up during training to bring other Columns up to strength

2nd Battalion The Burma Rifles
Lieutenant- Colonel L.G. Wheeler

Appendix B
Operation Thursday[302]
March – August 1944

Special Force - Order of Battle
Commander: Major General O. C. Wingate, DSO
(succeeded by Major-General W.D.A. Lentaigne).
Deputy Commander: Major – General G.W. Symes
(succeeded by Brigadier D. Tulloch)

3 (West African) Brigade ('Thunder')
Brigadier A.H Gillmore, succeeded by Brigadier A.H.G. Ricketts, DSO
Headquarters: 10 Column
6th Battalion Nigeria Regiment (6 NR): 39, 66 Columns

7th Battalion Nigeria Regiment (7 NR): 29, 35 Columns
12th Battalion Nigeria Regiment (12 NR): 12, 43 Columns

14 British Infantry Brigade (ex 70th Division) ('Javelin')
Brigadier Tom Brodie
Headquarters: 59 Column
1st Battalion The Beds & Herts Regiment: 16, 61 Columns

---

[302] Tony Redding, p. 85.

7th Battalion The Royal Leicestershire Regiment: 47, 74 Columns

2nd Battalion The Black Watch: 42, 73 Columns

2nd Battalion The York and Lancaster Regiment: 65, 84 Columns

5th Field Company, Royal Engineers: (Support)

16 British Infantry Brigade (ex 70th Division) ('Enterprise')

Brigadier Bernard Fergusson, DSO

Headquarters: 99 Column

51st/69th Field Regiments, Royal Artillery (as infantry) (51/69 RA): 51, 69 Columns

2nd Battalion The Queen's Royal Regiment (Queens): 21, 22 Columns

2nd Battalion The Royal Leicester Regiment: 17, 71 Columns

45th Reconnaisance Regiment, Royal Armoured Corp

(as infantry) (45 Recce): 45, 54 Columns

2nd Field Company, Royal Engineers: (Support)

23 British Infantry Brigade (ex 70th Division)

Brigadier Lance Perowne, CBE

Headquarters: 32 Column

60th Field Regiment, Royal Artillery (as infantry) (60 RA): 60, 68 Columns

2nd Battalion The Duke of Wellingtons Regiment: 33, 76 Columns

4th Battalion The Border Regiment: 34, 55 Columns

1st Battalion The Essex Regiment: 44, 56 Columns

12th Field Company Royal Engineers: (Support)

77 Indian Infantry Brigade ('Emphasis')

Brigadier Michael Calvert, DSO

Headquarters: 25 Column

1st Battalion The King's (Liverpool) Regiment (King's): 81, 82 Columns

1st Battalion The Lancashire Fusiliers: 20, 50 Columns

1st Battalion The South Staffordshire Regiment: 38, 80 Columns

3rd Battalion 6th Gurkha Rifles (6GR): 36, 63 Columns

3rd Battalion 9th Gurkha Rifles (9 GR): 57, 93 Columns

Mixed Field Company, Royal Engineers / Royal Indian Engineers: (Support)

142 Company, Hong Kong Volunteers: (Support)

111 Indian Infantry Brigade ('Profound')

Brigadier 'Joe' Lentaigne, CBE, DSO (succeeded by Lieutenant – Colonel Jack Masters, DSO, Brigade Commander)

Headquarters: 48   Column

2nd Battalion The Kings Own Royal Regiment (Kings Own): 41, 46 Column

1st Battalion The Cameronians: 26, 90 Column

3rd Battalion 4th Gurkha Rifles (4GR): 30 Column

Mixed Field Company, Royal Engineers / Royal Indian Engineers: (Support)

Morris Force

Brigadier J.R. Morris, CBE, DSO

4th Battalion 9th Gurkha Rifles (9GR): 49, 94 Column

3rd Battalion 4th Gurkha Rifles (4GR): 40 Column

Bladet Force
Major Blain
Commando Engineers

Dah Force
Lieutenant D.C. Herring
Kachin Levies

Other Units
2nd Battalion The Burma Rifles (Burrifs)
R, S, U Troops, 160th Jungle Field Regiment, Royal Artillery (25 pounders)
W, X, Y, Z Troops 69th Light Anti-Aircraft Regiment, Royal Artillery (Bofors)
1st Air Commando Group (USAAF) (Colonel Phil Cochran)

Bibliography

UNPUBLISHED PRIMARY SOURCES
Archives
The Churchill Archive, Cambridge
CHAR 20/157:   Prime Minister's Personal Telegram, Prime Minister to President No. 592, Reply to President's No. 479 and 480, 25 February 1944

CHAR 4/341: WSC to Sir Henry Pownall, Corrections: comments and queries on First Edition and proofs of Volume 5, on comment from Field Marshal Sir William Slim that the Fourteenth Army was not mentioned by name in Volume 5, Image 8 of 185

CHAR 20/211/36-38: Telegram   from   Lord   Louis Mountbatten to WSC marked "Personal" reporting on his visit to the Fourteenth Army Front in Burma: stating that he is confident of a major defeat of the Japanese in this area, in addition to the capture of Mandalay [Burma]; and emphasising the high morale and superiority of Allied forces. 23 January 1945

Combined Arms Research Library, Digital Library, Fort Leavenworth, KS
Casablanca Conference, January 1943, Papers & Minutes of Meetings 1943 (Washington, DC: Office of the Combined Chiefs of Staff, 1943)

Trident Conference, May 1943, Papers & Minutes of Meetings 1943 (Washington, DC: Office of the Combined Chiefs of Staff, 1943)

Quadrant Conference, August 1943, Papers & Minutes of Meetings 1943 (Washington, DC: Office of the Combined Chiefs of Staff, 1943)

Sextant Conference, November – December 1943, Papers & Minutes of Meetings 1943 (Washington, DC: Office of the Combined Chiefs of Staff, 1943)

Octagon Conference, September 1944, Papers & Minutes of Meetings 1944 (Washington, DC: Office of the Combined Chiefs of Staff, 1944)

Eastern Air Command, Weekly Intelligence Summary No. 10 (Calcutta: Headquarters Eastern Air Command, 3rd Nov 1944)

Foreign Relations of the United States: The Conferences at Washington and Quebec 1943 (Washington,DC: United States Government Printing Office, 1970)

IB Theatre Transportation N-9198 (Fort Leavenworth, KS: Combined Arms Research Library, May 1945)

Monthly Summary of Enemy Dispositions: Ground, Air, Navy – General Headquarters Southwest Pacific Area (Brisbane: General Headquarters Southwest Pacific Area, 31st March 1944)

Japanese Monograph 45, History of Imperial General Headquarters, Army Section (Tokyo: Headquarters United States Army, Japan, 1952; revised 1959)

Japanese Monograph 132, Burma Operations Record, 28th Army Organisation in Akyab Area (Tokyo: Headquarters United States Army, Japan 1952; revised 1958)

Japanese Monograph 134, Burma Operations Record, 15th Army Operations in Imphal Area and Withdrawal to Northern Burma (Revised Edition) (Tokyo: Headquarters United States Army, Japan Oct 1952; revised 1957)

Japanese Tactics in Burma Report, 9082 (New Delhi: Joint Intelligence Collection Agency, October 1944)

Tactics and Strategy of the Japanese Army in the Burma Campaign from November 1943 – September 1944, JICA/ CBI/ SEA Report No. 9082 (New Delhi: Joint Intelligence Collection Agency, November 1944)

Imperial War Museum, London

Box No. 82/15/1: Private Papers of Major General G. W. Symes CBMC, Diary 6 November 1943 – 11th April 1944

Cat No. 9942: Brigadier Michael Calvert ,Oral Interview, Reel 18

Misc. 54, Item 824: Field Marshal Viscount Slim to Lt. Col. H R K Gibbs, Commentary notes for page 131, from Slim on Gibbs draft narrative of 6th Gurkha Rifles, 3 pages, 14 July 1952. Field Marshal Viscount Slim to Lt. Col. H R K Gibbs, 1942-1963

National Archives & Records Administration, Washington

Franklin D. Roosevelt Library and Museum Website; version date 2016

Map Room Papers, Box 25: Conferences: Strategic Studies, Vol.2, Prepared by JCS: Japan-Torch Follow-Up

Map Room Papers, Box 10: Exchange of Dispatches Between President Roosevelt and Generalissimo Chiang Kai Shek, 1941-42

Map Room Papers, Box 10: Exchange of Dispatches Between President Roosevelt and Generalissimo Chiang Kai Shek, 1943

Map Room Papers, Box 2: Churchill to Roosevelt, May – July 1942, Vol. 2

Map Room Papers, Box 2: Roosevelt to Churchill, August – October 1942

Map Room Papers, Box 5: Roosevelt to Churchill February 1944

The National Archives, Kew

Cabinet Office Papers

CAB 101/ 184: Wingate papers, 1943-45, 1958

CAB 101/ 185: Slim comments to Kirby, Chapter XIV, General Remarks, p.5, 22 October 1958

CAB 101/105: War Cabinet and Cabinet Office: Historical Section: War Histories (Second World War), Vol.II, Preliminary draft: part 1

CAB 101/181: Correspondence with Earl Mountbatten of Burma, Supreme Allied Commander, South East Asia, 1943-1946, 1958-1960

CAB 106/206: Comments on the narrative on operations of Special Force (second Wingate Expedition) by the Force and Brigade Commanders and Field Marshal Sir William Slim, 1953

Premier Files

PREM 3/143/8: Plans for 1944 Campaign, Far East: Anakim, 1943

Records of the Fighting Services

AIR 2/7990: OPERATIONS: Far East (Code B, 55/2/2): Operation `Thursday': Report, 1944

AIR 23/1944: First Wingate Expedition: notes by the C.-in-C. India and report by Commander of IV Corps, 1943

AIR 23/1945: Operation 'Thursday', 1944

AIR 23/2709: Special Force: General Wingate's plan, 1944

AIR 23/7655: Operation 'Thursday': Allied landings in N.E. Burma, 1944

WO 106/4827: Japanese views on Brigadier O. C. Wingate's expeditions of 1943-1944 by Major General Symes, 1946

WO 203/1829: 77 Indian Infantry Brigade of 3rd Indian Division, Operations in Burma, February – August 1944

WO 203/4620: Operation 'Thursday' special force airborne

operation: report prepared by Brigadier General Staff of Special Force, 1944

<u>United States Air Force Historical Research Agency, Maxwell AFB, Alabama</u>

Colonel Philip G. Cochran, US Air Force Oral History Interview,   1975
<http://www.afsoc.af.mil/Portals/86/documents/history/AFD-070330-008.pdf>

Unpublished Papers
Albert C. Wedemeyer, 'German General Staff School' (Report to Military Intelligence Division, War Department, August 1938)

J.D. Atwell, M.O., 6 Field Ambulance, West Africa Army Medical Corps, 81st West African Division

Oral Histories
Private Richard Day, Royal Welch Fusiliers, 1944, Personal Interview, 1 February 2018

Private Thomas Parker, Bren Gunner, 1st Battalion, The Cameronians, 90th Column, 111 Brigade, 1944, Personal Interview, 23 January 2018

PUBLISHED PRIMARY SOURCES: OFFICIAL PUBLICATIONS
Arnold, Henry H., *Second Report of the Commanding General of the Army Air Forces to the Secretary of War* (Washington DC: United States Army Air Forces, 1945)

Japanese Monograph 64, Record of the Air Operation in Burma Jan 9142-Aug 1945 (Tokyo: 1st Demobilization Bureau, 1946)

Jungle Warfare: War Department Field Manual FM 72-20

US War Department (Washington: United States Government Printing Office, Oct 1944)

Mountbatten of Burma, Vice Admiral the Earl, KG PC GCSI GCIE GCVO KCB DSO, *Report to the Combined Chiefs of Staff by the Supreme Allied Commander South East Asia, 1943-1945* (London: HMSO, 1951)

Owen, Lieut. – Colonel Frank, O.B.E., *The Campaign in Burma: Prepared for South East Asia Command by the Central Office of Information* (London: HMSO, 1946)

Trager, Frank, *Burma: Japanese Military Administration: selected documents, 1941-1945* (Philadelphia: University of Pennsylvania, 1971)

Wingate, Brigadier Orde C., *Report on Operations of 77th Indian Infantry Brigade in Burma February –June 1943* (New Delhi: Government of India Press, 1943)

War with Japan Part 1 (WestPoint, NY: Command and General Staff College, 1947)

War with Japan Part 2 (WestPoint, NY: Command and General Staff College, 1947)

PUBLISHED PRIMARY SOURCES: DIARIES & MEMOIRS

Alanbrooke, Field Marshal Lord, *War Diaries 1939-45* (London: Weidenfeld & Nicolson, 2001)

Baines, Frank, *Chindit Affair: A Memoir of the War in Burma*, Kindle Edition (Barnsley: Pen & Sword, 2011)

Bond, Brian, ed., *Chief of Staff: The Diaries of Lieutenant-General Sir Henry Pownall*, 2 vols (London: Leo Cooper, 1974)

Calvert, Michael, *Fighting Mad: One Man's Guerrilla War* (London: Jarrolds, 1964; repr. 2004)

Calvert, Michael, *Prisoners of Hope* (London: Jonathan Cape, 1952; repr. 1971)

Carfrae, Charles, *Chindit Column* (London: Harper Collins, 1985)

Churchill, Winston S., *The Second World War* Abridged Single Volume Edition (London: Cassell 1959; repr.1965)

Churchill, Winston S., *The Second World War*, 6 vols (London: Cassell, 1952; repr. Folio Society, 2000)

Danchev, Alex, *Establishing the Anglo-American Alliance: The Second World War Diaries of Brigadier Vivian Dykes* (London: Brasseys, 1990)

Fergusson, Bernard, *Beyond the Chindwin* (London: Collins, 1945; repr. 2009)

Fergusson, Bernard, *The Wild Green Earth* (London: Collins, 1946; repr. 2015)

Fergusson, Brig. Bernard, 'Upper Burma, 1943-44', *The Geographical Journal*, 107/1/2 (Jan.-Feb. 1946), 1-10

Grehan, John & Martin Mace, *Despatches from the Front: The Commanding Officers' Reports from the Field and at Sea, The Battle for Burma 1943-45, from Kohima & Imphal Through to Victory* (Barnsley: Pen & Sword, 2015)

Hedley, Maj. John, *Jungle Fighter: Infantry Officer, Chindit & S.O.E. Agent in Burma, 1943-45* (Brighton: Tom Donovan Publishing, 1996)

Huston, Maj. General John W., ed., *American Airpower Comes of Age: General Henry H. 'Hap' Arnold's World War II Diaries*, 2 vols (Montgomery, AL: Air University Press, 2002)

Ismay, General the Lord, *The Memoirs of Lord Ismay* (London: Heinemann, 1960)

James, Harold, *Across the Threshold of Battle: Behind Japanese Lines with Wingate's Chindits, Burma 1943* (Lewes: The Book Guild, 1993)

MacDonald Fraser, George, *Quartered Safe out Here* (London: Harvill, 1992)

Marshall, General George Catlett, *The Papers of George Catlett Marshall*, 7 vols (Baltimore and London: The Johns Hopkins University Press, 1996)

Masters, John, *The Road Past Mandalay* (London: Michael Joseph, 1961; repr. 2002)

Mountbatten, Admiral The Lord Louis, *Personal Diary of Admiral the Lord Louis Mountbatten, 1943-46*, ed. By Philip Ziegler (London: Collins, 1988)

O'Brien, Terence, *Out of the Blue: A Pilot with the Chindits* (London: Collins, 1984)

Peterson, A. H., G. C. Reinhardt & E. E. Conger, eds, 'Symposium on the Role of Airpower in Counterinsurgency and Unconventional Warfare: Chindit Operations in Burma', *United States Air Force Project Rand* (Santa Monica CA: The Rand Corporation, 1963)

Randall, John, *Battle Tales from Burma* (Barnsley: Pen & Sword, 2004)

Rhodes James, Richard, *Chindit* (London: John Murray, 1980)

Rolo, Charles J., *Wingate's Raiders: an Account of the Fabulous Adventure That Raised the Curtain on the Battle for Burma*, (London: George G. Harrap, 1944)

Shaw, Jesse, *Special Force : A Chindit's Story* (Gloucester: Alan Sutton, 1986)

Shaw, James, *The March Out* (London: Rupert Hart-Davis, 1953)

Slim, Field Marshal Viscount, *Defeat into Victory* (London: Cassell, 1956; repr. 2009)

Stilwell, General Joseph W., *The Stilwell Papers: Iconoclastic Account of America's Adventures in China Ed. by Theodore H. White* (New York: De Capo, 1991)

Thompson, Sir Robert, KBE, *Make for the Hills* (London: Pen

& Sword, 1989)

Towill, Bill, *A Chindit's Chronicle* (New York: Authors Choice Press, 1990)

Tulloch, Derek, *Wingate in Peace and War* (London: MacDonald, 1972)

Wedemeyer, Albert C., *Wedemeyer Reports* (New York: Holt, 1958)

PUBLISHED PRIMARY SOURCES:
CONTEMPORARY NEWSPAPERS AND JOURNALS

Air Commando H.Q., 'Second Air Invasion in Burma', *Daily Mail*, 10th April 1944

Arnold, General Henry H., 'The Aerial Invasion of Burma', *National Geographic* 86, August 1944, pp.129-148

Christian, John L., 'Burma: Strategic and Political', *Far Eastern Survey*, 11/3 (9 Feb. 1942), 40-44

Farley, Miriam S., 'Political Strategy Needed', *Far Eastern Survey*, 12/18 (8 Sept. 1943), 177-178

Gander, L. Marsland, 'British Jungle Force Kept Japanese on the Run', *Daily Telegraph*, 21 May 1943

Headquarters, SEAC, 'Chindit Columns in Action', *Times*, 4 May 1944

Hendershot, Clarence, 'The Liberation of Burma', *Pacific Historical Review*, 13/3 (Sep.1944), 271-277

Martin, Lt.-Gen. H., 'General Wingate Killed in Burma Plane Crash', *Daily Telegraph,* 1 April 1944

'Memorial to General Wingate', *Times*, 21 July 1944

Moore, Martin, 'Secret Allied March in Burma Jungle', *Daily Telegraph*, 15 March 1944

Moore, Martin, 'Wingate Leads Airborne Troops in Burma', *Daily Telegraph,* 27 March 1944

Nicholson, W. A., 'Wingate Killed in Air Crash', *Daily Mail*, 1 April 1944

Official Statement, 'Airborne Troops Reinforced', *Times*, 25 April 1944

Our Correspondent, 'North Burma Offensive', *Times*, 18 May 1944

Our Own Correspondent, 'New Tactics in Burma, Airborne Forces Behind Enemy', *Times,* 18 March 1944

Our Own Correspondent, 'Storming of Mogaung', *Times*, 29 June 1944

Our Special Correspondent, 'Chindits Feats of Arms', *Times*, 28 June 1944

Sabben-Clare, E.E., 'African Troops in Asia', *African Affairs*, 44/177 (Oct. 1945), 151-157

Sewell, Horace S., 'The Campaign in Burma', *Foreign Affairs*, 23/3 (Apr. 1945), 496-504

Special Correspondent, 'Commando in the Jungle, Raids into Burma', *Times,* 21 May 1943

Special Correspondent, 'Mastery in the Jungle', *Times,* 30 June 1943

Special Correspondent, 'Wingate Wrecking Expedition in Burma', *Times*, 24 May 1943

Stanford, Graham, 'Battle "Honours" for the Chindits', *Daily Mail*, 17 June 1944

'VC for Officer Who Used a Sword', *Times*, 21 May 1949

PUBLISHED SECONDARY SOURCES: BOOKS AND MONOGRAPHS

Allen, Louis, *Burma: The Longest War, 1941-45* (London: J.M Dent, 1984; repr. 1986)

Anglim, Simon, 'Major General Orde Wingate's Chindit Operations in World War II: Historical Case Study for the

Operating without a Net Project', in *Strategic Analysis Assessments* (Reading: University of Reading, 2009)

<https://www.academia.edu/647651/Major General Orde Wingates Chindit Operations in World War II - Historical Case Study for the Operating without a Net Project>

Anglim, Simon James, 'Orde Wingate & the British Army 1922-1944: Military Thought & Practice Compared & Contrasted' (unpublished doctoral thesis, University of Wales, 2007)

Anglim, Simon, *Orde Wingate: Unconventional Warrior - from the 1920s to the Twenty-First Century* (Barnsley: Pen & Sword, 2014)

Athens, Maj. Arthur J., 'The Directional Megaphone a Theatre Commander Uses to Communicate his Vision and Intent: Mountbatten & SEAC' (Fort Leavenworth, KS: US Army Command & General Staff College, 1993)

Atkins, Maj John, RLC, 'A Model for Modern Non-Linear, Non Contiguous Operations: The War in Burma 1943-45' (Fort Leavenworth, KS: School of Advanced Military Studies, United States Army Command & General Staff College, 2003)

Bidwell, Shelford, *The Chindit War: Stilwell, Wingate, and the Campaign in Burma: 1944* (New York: MacMillan, 1979)

Bierman, John and Smith, Colin, *Fire in the Night: Wingate of Burma, Ethiopia, and Zion* (London: MacMillan, 1999)

Bond, Brian, Editor & Tachikawa, Kyoichi, Series Editor, *British and Japanese Military Leadership in the Far East War 1941-45* (Abingdon: Routledge, 2012)

Brower, Charles F., *Defeating Japan: The Joint Chiefs of Staff and Strategy in the Pacific War, 1943-1945* (New York: Palgrave Macmillan, 2012)

Bull, Dr. Stephen, *World War II Jungle Warfare Tactics*

(Oxford: Osprey, 2007)

Cain, Major Gregory M., 'Air Leadership in Joint/Combined Operations: Lt. General George E. Stratemeyer of the Eastern Air Command, 1943-1945' (Montgomery, AL: School of Advanced Airpower Studies, 1999)

Callahan, Raymond A., *Burma: 1942-45* (Cranbury, NJ: Associated University Presses, 1979)

Callwell, Charles E., *Small Wars: Their Principles and Practice,* New Rev edition (London: Watchmaker Publishing, 2010)

Calvert, Michael, *Chindits: Long Range Penetration* (London: Macmillan, 1974)

Chapman, James, *British Comics: A Cultural History* (London: Reaktion Books, 2011)

Chapman, James, *The British at War: Cinema, State and Propaganda, 1939-45* (London: Tauris, 1998)

Chinnery, Philip D., *March or Die: The Story of Wingate's Chindits* (Shrewsbury: Airlife, 1997)

Coltrane, William L., 'Orde Wingate's Chindits: Burma LRP' (Lubbock, TX: Texas Tech. University, 1987)

Cox, LCDR Samuel J, USN., 'The China Theatre, 1944-1945: A failure of Joint and Combined Operations Strategy' (Fort Leavenworth KS: Faculty of the US Army Command & General Staff College, 1993)

Dewaters, Diane K., 'The World War II Conferences in Washington D.C. and Quebec City: Franklin D. Roosevelt and Winston S. Churchill' (Arlington, TX: University of Texas at Arlington, 2008)

Diamond, Jon, *Stilwell and the Chindits: The Allied Campaign in Northern Burma 1943 – 1944, Images of War* (Barnsley: Pen & Sword, 2015)

Ehrman, John, *Grand Strategy Vol. V: August 1943 –*

September 1944, HMSO Official History of the Second World War, 6 vols (London: HMSO, 1956)

Fergusson, Bernard, *The Watery Maze: The Story of Combined Operations* (London: Collins, 1961)

Hamilton, John A. L., *War Bush: 81 (West African) Division in Burma 1943-45* (Norwich: Michael Russell, 2001)

Hargreaves, Andrew Lennox, 'The Analysis of the Rise, Use, Evolution and Value of Anglo-American Commando and Special Force Formations 1939-1945' (London: Kings College, 2009)

Hastings, Max, *Nemesis: The Battle for Japan, 1944-45* (London: Harper Press, 2007; repr. 2014)

Hastings, Max, *Finest Years: Churchill as Warlord 1940-45* (London: Harper Press, 2009)

Hawley, Dennis, *The Death of Wingate & Subsequent Events* (Braunton: Merlin Books, 1994)

Hayes, Grace Person, *The History of the Joint Chiefs of Staff in World War 2: The War Against Japan* (Annapolis: United States Naval Institute Press, 1982)

Heuser, Beatrice, *The Evolution of Strategy: Thinking War from Antiquity to the Present* (Cambridge: University Press, 2010)

Holland, James, *Burma '44: The Battle That Turned Britain's War in the East* (Corgi, London, 2017)

Howard, Michael, *Grand Strategy Vol. IV: August 1942 – September 1943, HMSO Official History of the Second World War,* 6 vols (London: HMSO, 1970)

Ienega, Saburo, *Japans Last War: World War II and the Japanese, 1931-1945 (Oxford: Blackwell, 1979)*

Johnson, Benjamin J., 'From Burma to Berlin: The Development of U.S. Air Transport 1938-1949' (Lincoln NE: University of Nebraska, 2014)

Lacey, James, *Keep From All Thoughtful Men,* (Annoplis, MD: Naval Institute Press, 2011)

Keane, Fergal, *Road of Bones, The Epic Siege of Kohima 1944* (London: Harper Press, 2010)

Keegan, John, ed., *Churchill's Generals* (London: Cassell, 2005)

Kirby, Maj. Gen. S. Woodburn, *The War Against Japan,* 5 vols (London: HMSO 1958; repr. 2004)

Latimer, Jon, *Burma: The Forgotten War* (London: John Murray, 2004)

Larrabee, Eric, *Commander in Chief: Franklin Delano Roosevelt, His Lieutenants and Their War* (New York: Harper & Row, 1987; repr. 1988)

Liddell Hart, Basil, *Strategy* (London: Faber & Faber, 1954; repr. 1991)

Liddell Hart, Basil, *History of the Second World War* (London: Weidenfeld & Nicolson, 1970)

Lyman, Robert, *Slim, Master of War: Burma, 1942-5: Burma and the Birth of Modern Warfare* (London: Constable & Robinson, 2004)

Matloff, Maurice, *Strategic Planning for Coalition Warfare 1943-44* (Washington DC: Department of the Army, Centre for Military History, 1958; repr. 1994)

McKeeman, Maj. Michael W., 'Unconventional Warfare at the Operational Level: The Chindits in Burma in WWII' (Fort Leavenworth, KS: School of Advanced Military Studies, United States Army Command & General Staff College, 1988)

McLaughlin, John J., *General Albert C. Wedemeyer: America's Unsung Strategist in World War II* (Philadelphia: Casement, 2013, Kindle Edition)

McLynn, Frank, *The Burma Campaign: Disaster into Triumph 1942-45* (London: Random House, 2011)

McMichael, Major Scott R., 'A Historical Perspective on

Light Infantry' (Fort Leavenworth KS: Combat Studies Institute, United States Army Command & General Staff College, 1987)

Mansoor, Peter R., and Murray, Williamson, (Eds.), *Grand Strategy and Military Alliances,* (Cambridge: University Press, 2016)

Mead, Peter, *Orde Wingate and the Historians* (Braunton: Merlin, 1987)

Miller, Russell, *Uncle Bill: The Authorised Biography of Field Marshal Viscount Slim* (London: Weidenfeld & Nicolson, 2013)

Moreman, Tim, *Chindit 1942-45* (Oxford: Osprey, 2009)

Moreman, Tim, *The Jungle, Japanese and the British Commonwealth Armies at War, 1941-45: Fighting Methods, Doctrine and Training for Jungle Warfare* (Abingdon: Routledge, 2014)

Mori, Tokato, 'Co-Prosperity or Commonwealth? Japan, Britain and Burma 1940-1945' (unpublished doctoral thesis, London School of Economics, 2006)

Moynahan, Brian, *Jungle Soldier: The True Story of Freddy Spencer Chapman* (London: Quercus, 2009)

Mosley, Leonard, *Gideon Goes to War* (London: Arthur Barker, 1955)

Nath, Colonel Prithvi, VSM, *Wingate: His Relevance to Contemporary Warfare* (New Delhi: Sterling, 1990)

Pearson, Michael, *The Burma Air Campaign 1941-1945* (Barnsley: Pen & Sword, 2006)

Pogue, Forrest C., *George C. Marshall,* 4 vols (New York: Viking Press, 1966)

Redding, Tony, *War in the Wilderness: The Chindits in Burma 1943-44* (Stroud: The History Press, 2011)

Romanus, Charles F. & Riley Sunderland, *Stilwell's Mission to China* (Washington: Dept. of the Army, 1953)

Romanus, Charles F. & Riley Sunderland, *Stilwell's Command Problems: United States Army in World War II: China-Burma-India Theatre* (Washington: Dept. of the Army, 1956)

Romanus, Charles F. & Riley Sunderland, *Time Runs Out in CBI* (Washington: Dept. of the Army, 1959)

Rooney, David, *Burma Victory: Imphal, Kohima and the Chindit Issue, March 1944 to May 1945* (London: Arms & Armour, 1992)

Rooney, David, *Wingate and the Chindits: Redressing the Balance* (London: Arms and Armour, 1994)

Rooney, David, *Mad Mike: A Life of Brigadier Michael Calvert* (Barnsley: Leo Cooper, 1997)

Rooney, David, *Stilwell the Patriot: Vinegar Joe, the Brits & Chiang Kai Shek* (Barnsley, Pen & Sword, 2005)

Royle, Trevor, *Orde Wingate: A Man of Genius 1903-1944* (London: Weidenfeld & Nicolson, 1995; repr. 2010)

Salmi, Lt. Col. Derek M., 'Slim Chance: The Pivotal Role of Air Mobility in the Burma Campaign' (Montgomery AL: Air University Press, 2014)

Schofield, Victoria, *Wavell: Soldier and Statesman* (London: John Murray, 2006)

Sharp, Brandon, 'Cooperation & Sacrifice: How Divergent Allied Objectives, Interests, and End States Sowed the Seeds of Failure in the China-Burma-India Theatre' (Washington D.C.: Georgetown University, 2013)

Shores, Christopher F., *Air War for Burma,* 3 vols (London: Grub Street, 2005)

Smith, Brig. Eric D., *Battle for Burma* (London: B.T. Batsford Limited, 1979)

Stoler, Mark A., *Allies and Adversaries: The Joint Chiefs of*

Staff, The Grand Alliance, and U.S. Strategy in World War II (Chapel Hill: University of North Carolina Press, 2000)

Stoler, Mark A., *Allies in War: Britain and America Against the Axis Powers 1940-1945* (London: Hodder Arnold, 2005)

Strachan, Hew, *The Direction of War: Contemporary Strategy in Historical Perspective* (Cambridge: Cambridge University Press, 2013)

Sykes, Christopher H., *Orde Wingate* (London: Collins, 1959)

Taylor, Dr Joe G., 'Air Supply in the Burma Campaigns' (Montgomery, AL: USAF Historical Division, 1957)

Thomas, Lowell, *Back to Mandalay* (New York: The Greystone Press, 1951)

Thompson, Julian, *Forgotten Voices of Burma* (London: Ebury Press, 2009)

Thompson, Julian, *The Imperial War Museum Book of the War in Burma 1942-1945* (London: Pan 2002)

Thompson, Julian, *The Imperial War Museum Book of War Behind Enemy Lines* (London: Sidgwick & Jackson, 1998; repr. 1999)

Thorburn, Gordon, *Jocks in the Jungle: The Black Watch and Cameronians as Chindits* (Barnsley: Pen & Sword, 2012)

Thorne, Christopher, *Allies of a Kind* (London: Hamish Hamilton, 1978)

Torres, John J. 'Historical Analysis of 1st Air Commando Group Operations in the CBI Theatre August 1943-May 1944' (Montgomery, AL: Air University, Air Command and Staff College, March 1997)

Tuchman, Barbara, *Stilwell and the American Experience in China, 1911-45* (New York: MacMillan, 1970)

VanWagner, R.D., '1st Air Commando Group, Any Place, Any Time, Any Where' (Montgomery, AL: Air Command & Staff College, 1986)

Watt, D. Cameron, *Succeeding John Bull: America in*

Britain's Place 1900-1975: Wiles Lectures Given at the Queen S University of Belfast (Cambridge: University Press, 1984; repr. 2008)

Weiss, Steve, *Allies in Conflict: Anglo-American Strategic Negotiations, 1938-44: Studies in Military and Strategic History* (London: Palgrave Macmillan, 1996)

Y'Blood, William T., *Air Commandos against Japan: Allied Special Operations in WW II Burma* (Annapolis, MD: Naval Institute Press, 2008)

Ziegler, Philip, *Mountbatten: The Official Biography* (London: Book Club Associates, 1985)

PUBLISHED SECONDARY SOURCES: ARTICLES AND ESSAYS

Agbi, S. Olu, 'The Pacific War Controversy in Britain: Sir Robert Craigie versus The Foreign Office', *Modern Asian Studies*, 17/3 (1983), 489-517

Allen, Louis, 'Japanese Intelligence Systems, Intelligence Services During the Second World War Part 2' , *Journal of Contemporary History* 22/4 (October 1987), 547-562

Anglim, Simon, 'Orde Wingate and the Theory Behind the Chindit Operations: Some Recent Findings', *RUSI,* (April 2002) 92-98

Anglim, Simon, '77 Brigade and Orde Wingate's Real Heirs', *RUSI,* (30 March 2015)
<https://rusi.org/commentary/77-brigade-and-orde-wingate%E2%80%99s-real-heirs>

Anglim, Simon, 'Orde Wingate, 'Guerrilla' Warfare and Long-Range Penetration, 1940-44', *Academia.edu* (2016)
<https://www.academia.edu/645950/Orde_Wingate_Guerrilla Warfare_and_Long-range_Penetration_1940_44>

Bidwell, Shelford, 'Wingate and the Official Historians: An

Alternative View', *Journal of Contemporary History*, 15/2 (April 1980), 245-256

Booth, Christopher, L'Etang, H.J.C.J., and Ober, William B. et.al., 'A Question of Confidence', *British Medical Journal, Clinical Research Edition,* 288/6414 (February 1984), 398-400

Callahan, Dr. Raymond, 'Orde Wingate and the Historians.' By Peter Mead, Book Review, *The American Historical Review*, 93/4 (October 1988), 1056

Callahan, Dr. Raymond, 'What Churchill Left Out', Mason Lecture, National WWII Museum, New Orleans (10 September 2011) <http://www.nationalww2museum.org/learn/public-programming/lectures/raymond-callahan.html>

Callahan, Dr. Raymond, 'The Strange Case of the Prime Minister and the Fighting Prophet', The Churchill Centre, *Finest Hour,* 139 (Summer 2008), 36-39 <http://www.winstonchurchill.org/publications/finest-hour/finest-hour-139>

Cate, James Lea, 'Global Command: The Double Cross Bee Cee', The Journal of Modern History, 23/4 (December 1951), 335-342

Chan, K. C., 'The Abrogation of British Extraterritoriality in China 1942-43: A Study of Anglo-American-Chinese Relations', *Modern Asian Studies*, 11/ 2 (1977), 257-291

Charles, Patrick J., 'Historical Reflections on Air Commando Theory', *Air Commando Journal*,2/3 (Summer 2013), 9-13 <https://aircommando.org/sites/journal/air_commando_journal_082013.pdf>

Daugherty, Leo J. III, 'Supplying War: Inter-Service and Inter-Allied Cooperation in China-Burma-India', *Joint Forces Quarterly* (Summer 1996), 95-105
< http://www.dtic.mil/dtic/tr/fulltext/u2/a426697.pdf>

Gibbs, Ashleigh, 'Lost Patrol', *Commando Comics*, 4820

(August 1965), 1-63

Greene, Fred, 'The Military View of American National Policy, 1904-1940', *The American Historical Review*, 66/2 (January 1961), 354-377

Harrison, Richard A., 'Testing the Water: A Secret Probe Towards Anglo-American Military Co-operation in 1936', *The International History Review*, 7/2 (May 1985), 214-234

Hess, Gary R., 'Franklin Roosevelt and Indochina', *The Journal of American History*, 59/2 (September 1972), 353-368

Jacobsen, Mark H., 'Winston Churchill and the Third Front', *Pacific Coast Conference on British Studies* (March 1998)
<http://www.dtic.mil/dtic/tr/fulltext/u2/a195340.pdf>

Jensen, De Lamar, 'Allied Strategy in World War II: The Churchill Era, 1942-1943', Brigham Young University Studies, 5/1 (Autumn 1962) 49-63

Lacey, James, 'World War II's Real Victory Program', *Journal of Military History*, 75/3 (July 2011), 811-834

La Feber, Walter, 'Roosevelt, Churchill and Indochina: 1942-45', *The American Historical Review'*, 80/5 (December 1975), 1277-1295

Leighton, Richard M., 'Allied Unity of Command in the Second World War: A Study in Regional Military Organization', *Political Science Quarterly,* 67/3 (September 1952), 399-425

McLaughlin, John J., and Lomazow, Steven, 'Albert Coady Wedemeyer', and Lacey, James, 'Historical Truths and Tilting at Windmills', Counterpoint, *Journal of Military History,* 77/1 (January 2013), 255-72

Maga, Timothy P., 'Franklin Roosevelt and the Pacific War Council 1942-1944', *Presidential Studies Quarterly*, 21/2 (Spring 1971) 351-363

Mason, Herbert A., Bergeron, SSgt. Randy G. and Renfrow,

TSgt. James A. Jnr., USAFR 'Operation Thursday: Birth of the Air Commando' (Washington DC: Office of Air force History 1994)

Mason, Philip, 'The Chindit War: The Campaign in Burma 1944.' By Shelford Bidwell, Book Review, *International Affairs,* 56/3 (Summer 1980), 520-521

Mead, Peter and Bidwell, Shelford, 'Orde Wingate – Two Views', *Journal of Contemporary History*, 15/3 (July 1980), 401-404

Mead, Peter, 'Orde Wingate & the Official Historians', *Journal of Contemporary History*, 14/1 (January 1979), 55-82

Millett, John D., 'World War II: The Post-Mortem Begins', *Political Science Quarterly*, 61/3 (September 1946), 321-348

Morton, Louis, 'War Plan Orange: Evolution of a Strategy', *World Politics*, 11/2 (January 1959), 221-250

Officer, Maj. Gen. W. J., 'With Wingate's Chindits, A Record of Heedless Valor', Book 4, US Army Medical Department (Washington, DC: US Army Office of Medical History, Books and   Documents) http://history.amedd.army.mil/booksdocs/wwii/CrisisFleeting/bookfour.htm>

Rearden, Steven L., 'Council of War: A History of the Joint Chiefs of Staff 1942-91' (Washington DC: Joint History Office, NDU press, 2012)

Reynolds, David, 'From World War to Cold War: The Wartime Alliance and Post-War Transitions, 1941-1947', *The Historical Journal*, 45/1 (March 2002), 211-227

Rhodes James, Richard, 'Orde Wingate and the Historians.' By Peter Mead, Book Review, *Journal of Southeast Asian Studies*, 19/1 (March 1988), 164-165

Ritchie, Dr Sebastian, 'Rising from the Ashes: Allied Air Power and Air Support for the 14th Army in Burma 1943-45', *Royal Air force Historical Society Journal,* 32 (2003), 55-67

Roberts, Henry L., 'Gideon Goes to War', Book Reviews, *Foreign Affairs*, 34/4 (July 1956), 496-504

Romanus, Charles F., 'Stilwell and the American Experience in China 1911-1945.' By Barbara Tuchman, Book Review, The Journal of Asia Studies, 31/12 (February 1972) 400-402

Rooney, David, 'A Grave Injustice - Wingate and the Establishment', *History Today* (March 1994), 11-13

Sarantakes, Nicholas Evan, 'One Last Crusade: The British Pacific Fleet and its Impact on the Anglo-American Alliance', *The English Historical Review*, 121/491 (April 2006), 429-466

Sbrega, John J., 'Determination versus Drift: The Anglo-American Debate over the Trusteeship Issue, 1941-1945', *Pacific Historical Review,* 55/2 (May 1986), 256-280

Sbrega, John J., 'The Anticolonial Policies of Franklin D. Roosevelt: A Reappraisal', *Political Science Quarterly*, 101 (1986), 65-84

Sbrega, John J., "First Catch Your Hare": 'Anglo –American Perspectives on Indochina during the Second World War', *Journal of South East Asian Studies*, 14/1 (March 1983), 63-78

Sbrega, John J., 'The Japanese Surrender: Some Unexpected Consequences in Southeast Asia', *Asian Affairs*, 7 (Sept.-Oct. 1979), 45-63

Stein, Harold, 'An Adminstrative Tangle: The China Tangle, The American Effort in China from Pearl Harbour to the Marshall Mission.' By Herbert Feiss, Book Review, *World Politics*, 6/3 (April 1954), 378-393

Stoler, Mark A., 'The "Pacific First" Alternative in American World War II Strategy', *The International History Review*, 2/3 (July 1980) 432-452

Sunderland, Riley, 'The Secret Embargo', *Pacific Historical Review*, 29/1 (February 1960), 75-80

Thorne, Christopher, 'Indochina and Anglo-American

Relations, 1942-1945', *Pacific Historical Review*, 45/1 (February 1976), 73-96

Trager, Frank N., 'The Chindits and Marauders in Wartime Burma, a Review', *Pacific Affairs*, 34/1 (Spring 1961), 62-66

Vinacke, Harold, 'Report to the Combined Chiefs of Staff by SAC, SEAC, 1943-1945.' By Earl Mountabatten of Burma, and 'The Rise and Fall of the Japanese Empire.' By David H. James, Book Review, The Journal of Modern History, 25/1 (March 1953), 88-89

Whyte, Desmond, 'Medicine and War - A Trying Chindit', *British Medical Journal, Clinical Research Edition,* 285/6357 (December 1982), 176-180

Wingate, Sybil, 'Orde Wingate and His Critics', *The Spectator,* (29 May 1959), 760-762

Xu, Guangqiu , 'The Issue of US Air Support for China during the Second World War', *Journal of Contemporary History*, 36/3 (July 2001), 459-484

PUBLISHED SECONDARY SOURCES: FILM AND TELEVISION

'It's a Lovely Day Tomorrow: Burma 1942-43'*, The World at War*, Part 2, Disc 2 [DVD] (London: Thames TV, 1973)

Orde Wingate [DVD] (London: BBC, 1976)

ONLINE RESOURCES

Chindits Old Comrades Association;
http://www.chindits.info/COCA/history.htm